LITERATURE INSIDE OUT

TEN SPECULATIVE ESSAYS

LITERATURE
INSIDE
OUT

TEN
SPECULATIVE
ESSAYS

By *Frederic Will*

1966
THE PRESS OF
WESTERN RESERVE UNIVERSITY
Cleveland

Some of the essays included in this book appeared first in period-icals (sometimes in slightly different form), and the permission of their editors to reprint here is gratefully acknowledged. "From Naming to Fiction-Making" appeared in *Giornale di Metafisica*, XIII (1958), 569–83; "Heidegger and the Gods of Poetry" in *The Personalist*, XLIII (1962), 157–67; "Palamas, Lorca, and the Ques-tion of Tropes in Literature" in *Comparative Literature Studies*, I (1964), 133–42; "Aristotle and the Question of Character in Literature" in *The Review of Metaphysics*, XIV (1960), 353–59; "Sartre and the Question of Character in Literature" in *PMLA*, LXXVI (1961), 455–60; and "Aristotle and the Source of the Artwork" in *Phronesis*, V (1960), 1–17.

For Henri Peyre

TABLE OF CONTENTS

PART I

1. From Naming to Fiction-Making, *3*
2. Literature and Knowledge, *16*
3. Heidegger and the Gods of Poetry, *25*

PART II

4. Psychoanalysis and the Study of Ancient Greek Literature, *39*
5. Palamas, Lorca, and the Question of Tropes in Literature, *54*
6. Odysseus the Hero, *71*

PART III

7. Aristotle and the Question of Character in Literature, *85*
8. Sartre and the Question of Character in Literature, *94*

PART IV

9. Literature Inside Out, *113*
10. Aristotle and the Source of the Artwork, *118*

INTRODUCTION

These essays advance in a dramatic pattern. They move in first on literature as a body, an embodiment of truth *in the world*; as dependent for its essential strength on knowledge *drawn in*, essentialized. Then literature is seen, and "essayed," as the product of authors' psyches; as product of a movement from an inner, rather than an outer, source. In this perspective literature appears translucent, its inner structure temporarily revealing itself as an objectified pattern of human psychic needs. This translucency begins to thicken, though, with the slow transformation of the psychic into the "characterful." The argument thickens, simultaneously, to a difficult question: how is character, in literature, related to the character of its makers? At last the robes of "character" fall. The original substantiality of literature, as a body made somehow of and like the body of the outer world, is again restored. By now it is in a new guise: as a substantial body produced in words by imagination, from the whole of human experience.

To say that only selected scenes have been shown, from this drama, would be to say too little. My particular literary texts have been picked from far and wide: no effort has been made to fill the blanks between, or even to mention the blanks. Homer, Herondas, Palamas, Lorca, Heidegger, Sartre, Adrian Stokes, and Melanie Klein are among the best filled outlines. All provide what are here central examples of literature, or suggest ways to think toward literature. Through these movements, I believe, a growing argument occurs: both the cognitive and "ethical" values of literature let themselves be regularly advanced. That regularity is the book's chief guarantee of unity. But it must speak for itself, not simply be announced.

Iowa City, Iowa   F. W.
January, 1966

ix

Part I

I

FROM NAMING
TO FICTION-MAKING

For the notion of giving something a name is the vastest generative idea that ever was conceived.
—SUSANNE LANGER

i

Naming is the substitution of sounding letters, names, for something else which is "meant" by them; objects, ideas, moods; and all the relationships among more or less static entities—bonds which verbs, adverbs, or prepositions express; in short, whatever mind encounters. Certain encounters, say with the supernatural or simply with tenuous secular moods, baffle language. But they simultaneously invite it. As mind encounters them it tries to convert them into words. It is teased into the effort. Poetry often results from such efforts; what baffles language can not only fall into the class of the named but is often the most valuable example of the class. I will refer to the entire class as "reality," here. Reality is that "outer," that realm lying beyond man, *after* it has been named. This is a primary or human sense of reality.

What about the word "meaning"? Naming is the substitution of a name for something else, the named, which is "meant" by the name. Meaning seems to be a bridge of being, constructed between name and named. Or, for that matter, be-

3

tween name and the supposedly named. If a man, seeing a bird, calls it a "flower," meaning—in the present sense—still unites this particular name and this particular named. The meaning-certified similarity in being between name and named is a simple dynamic fact, resulting from mind grasping the name and the named in a single intelligible mood.

This preliminary definition needs substance; a characterization of that intelligible and dynamic mood in which mind names. It is easy to define naming; but the definition becomes clear only when translated into process. Otherwise there is a special danger: of imagining, on the one hand, a careful, name-proposing intellect; and on the other a unitary, calm object awaiting a name. This danger is only a more extreme version of subtler forms of name-named dualism. Those descriptions of naming assume that "reality" is external to the naming relation we adopt toward it. Such a description is misleading; at least unless it makes clear that *unnamed* reality is a mere inchoate "outer." Reality in its primary sense is learned with names and gains distinctness and depth from being named; in that sense language is the creator of reality. Reality and language are interwoven from the outset in mind.

The dynamic event of naming is traditional, occupied with inherited letters, sounds, words, sentences. The traditional is usually the public. Yet in each person *this* event is a private encounter with still undifferentiated, "outerly" reality, reality in a secondary sense. The names which we give that reality have been used before, often in the combinations we choose. Yet each reuse of them is private: its tone and context having never occurred before. Language, and so reality, is for each of us perpetually being created.

Not only is naming a *private* encounter with the outer, but it is also a private *encounter* with it. As a child begins to learn his native language, passing beyond the mere mimicking stage, he simultaneously learns the world. He associates the word "dog" with specific dogs, the verb "to ache" with something

that happens in his stomach, the adjective "red" with the color
of his father's necktie. He takes less advantage than his parents
of the mobility of language, the range of things that the word
"red" points to. He makes little use or sense of abstract words
like "truth" or "goodness." Symbolism and metaphor are
closed to him. (So is humor, I think.) In his intercreation of
language and the particulars of the outer, he lives language as
evident encounter. This is the stage in primitive peoples' development which Edward Sapir characterizes, remarking on

the widespread feeling, particularly among primitive people, of
that virtual identity or close correspondence of word and thing
which leads to the magic of spells.

There is another reason for considering the case of children
here. It is true that in them the closeness of a name to its original model is strongly felt. Yet here there are distinct limits,
even with children: surely they do not have an inner sense-
image of, say, each noun's meaning, of the described tree, or
dress, or of the different described stages in the opening of a
door. I imagine that the other parts of speech—verbs, adverbs
—are as pale to the child as to his parents. Most words evoke
in even the particularizing mind only a vague, composite
sense-image. It is not long before a child associates with the
word "dog" merely the nebulous, scarcely sensible image of
several neighborhood dogs. Beyond this stage, words quickly
lose all but the faintest aroma of the named.

The encounter of names with what they name is tenuous.
At its most direct it produces, around the word, a sensuous
overtone which mimes the qualitites of the named. There is
no reason, though, why sense images of any kind need to be the
way for names to encounter what they name. The indicative,
or outward-pointing energy of language is as often directed
toward a fleeting state of mind or group of ideas as toward
discernible objects of sense: in those more evanescent cases
verbal encounter may be almost entirely unsensuous. In addition, even aroused "feeling" is part of every verbal en-

counter, a function of emotion without representative power. This shadowy accompaniment to the naming act is a decisive component of language in action.

So mere "encounter" by no means explains the whole work of naming. How are we to complete our account? The example of the child for whom the word "red" was fixed to the color of his father's necktie is again useful. For him, and from the first moment, a certain sense "aura" will surround that word "red," even when the word is used, say, as a mere sound in pure poetry. "Aura" is a vague notion: I mean a specific, but rough-outlined feeling of reference beyond the surrounded word. A child fixes the aura of a word in his first uses of it, but that aura can be deepened and clarified. Furthermore, as the child uses his words in sentences they will be blended with the other words around them. They may then retain only a vague feeling of direction beyond themselves, from their aura-state. This is enough to preserve their encountering quality, tenuously. In an image: the "outerly," name-robbed reality resounds like distant surf around the name which closely and intimately means it.

In the dynamic operation of language the relations of name to named are oblique. In all kinds of language in action—though in degrees varying from the most to the least sensuous —the named is present as an aura of the name and contributes an aura of linguistic otherness.

These terms may help with the original definition of naming: the substitution of sounding letters for something which is meant by them. A verbal sound means something by conveying an aura of that thing or thought or quality. As soon as this word is joined to others, is made part of syntax, its unique aura is qualified and dissipated. The word becomes an element in an organic whole which has its own refined "aural" worth.

Now we have come halfway into the question of what naming is. But only halfway. The tendency, the thrust of naming, is plainly *away* from what is named. This point has been implicit here, say in the necessity to create a theory of auras: a theory accounting for the *separation* between word and thing. This separative progress is everywhere obvious in the growth of the individual, in whom maturity and greater power with abstractions go together. It can be illustrated by the history of language. In the evolution of the first written languages, from Sumerian through Babylonian to Assyrian, there is change from pictographs to alphabet. Sumerian pictographs are stylized pictures of material things: cow, sun, river. In Babylonian the same pictographs are still used, but are frequently arranged into words solely according to the sounds which correspond to particular pictures. That is, the pictographs are used as sound-carriers. Then in Assyrian cuneiform-writing the same pictographs which the Babylonians used have become so stylized that they have lost their visible similarity to the cow or sun or river. These Assyrian letters are part of an alphabet and have lost all pictorial meaning. As the letters of the languages of the Fertile Crescent evolved, they moved from a more to a less direct representation of the nameable.

The development of alphabet out of pictograph is pregnant: lodged here is a potent impulse to create language which is released into its full, flexible power to name reality. This is not an impulse to drive off the aura-meaning which binds names to named: it is an impulse to make names, as far as possible, "essences" of what they name and all units or groupings of language into essences or unique areas of experience of reality.

"Essences" I use in a special sense, to suggest the least sensuous component of naming's semantic relation to what it names. The names made by mature language are new realities based on what they mean; in this sense they are "essences." They result from mind's insistent recall of the name-experienced outer to the non-sensuous focus of consciousness.

It is almost as if the language-making mind draws the

substance out of the experienced world and makes out of that same substance the new forms of its own significance. It would not need to follow, from this, that naming is an effort to purify or give additional meaning to the named. It means only that naming is a way in which mind is able to take possession of the named. Naming is a form of humanization.

This human motive propels the rhythm of naming. That rhythm draws into mind both the inner and outer experienced world, and displays that world essentially, without dissipating the aura of the world: without completely destroying the impact of previous encounter. This drawing up of named into name is the rhythm of naming. It is still the substitution of words for things which they mean; but it is that act captured in operation.

ii

The act of naming is rooted deeply in "human nature." Man learns reality, his own image of the outer, simultaneously with his language. It would be untrue to say that a child experiences only what he names. But it seems that he can only experience clearly, and in a context, that which he names. Similarly, whatever the child *does* name is decisively humanized. It can never slip back into otherness; and it forms a habit. Whatever unnamed the child thereafter sees he names or wants to name. He has verbal hunger. In the early stages of man's development, it must have been much as it is now with children. When man lacked language, or had only a rudimentary one, he must have been like any other higher animal, bathed by the sensual flux of a contourless, meaningless existence. Without developed language, furthermore, he could not have had a group memory: history would have been impossible. We call that period "prehistoric" in which man had no written records. Even the self-consciousness necessary for having a history required a written language.

Such evidence relates naming to fundamental development

in man. Without the power to name and to write we would have remained savages or children—more savage or childish than we are.

This general point merges into more intimate, inward evidence of the paradigm-character of language's rhythm. Not only is there reason to suppose that language should have this character, but the echoes of the rhythm of naming—its encountering, essentializing, creative power—can be picked up all through the expressions of the self. (Where, by "self," I mean the principle of unity in us, and by the unity of which self is principle I mean the different expressions of self, the continuum of our powers.)

The core of self, the theme of its efforts, is love. "Love," here, means the desire to bring the encountered "outer" in essential form back to the focus of consciousness. It is an acquisitive power, having its metaphysical grounding in the being's thirst for more being: in being's desire to turn the "outer" into the human-real, and so to increase. In this definition of "love" I include usual meanings of the word as primary hints; they point at the word's root meaning. Those usual meanings—in different ways—point at our desire to make the *outer* deeply *ours*. Raw, bodily love, raping its object into ecstatic closeness, must reconcile itself to quick separation, must feed itself on prurient images: it is driven to plant the beloved in the eye of inner vision. It wants to hold the "other." On the other hand, the most holding, inward love, Dante's for Beatrice, starves without an object to guarantee its idealizations. It needs repeatedly to find its lovable object. Both encounter and essentializing are required for these two primary expressions of love.

If the self is at core "love," the rhythm of that love will be displayed in all of the self's main operations. This may be shown here very briefly and with an eye to the main point: showing the *context* of naming in the self.

Even so, one qualification is necessary. Language itself is

involved in most of the expressions of self which can be mentioned in an attempt to see if their rhythms are like that of language. I overlook this problem, believing that language is not the *characteristic* driving force of these expressions.

The atmosphere of the loving self is that of a "lacking," and of an according striving to acquire the absent. From this interior situation emerge the ideals which self places before it: standards of moral, aesthetic, or rational behavior. Such ideals are examples of what might fill lacking, unrealized being. But they are more than that: as such, ideals would be like fantasies of physical joy cast by lust onto some inner screen. The distinction of these ideals is that they require increase of discipline, refinement of casual self, in short— whatever we think of their objective status—that they seem to require self-improvement. There is nothing accidental in this organic relation between ideals and self's change: ideals are projections of self into the region of possibility, a heroic effort of self to pull itself up by its own "self-straps."

As the self looks "upward," it confronts its ideal which it then returns to its own dynamic focus. The purity and generality of the ideal are brought back to the contingency and particularity of the self. The rhythm of love is rehearsed in this acquisitive glance toward the heavens.

It is rehearsed similarly in another glance: the glance at nature. In practice both artist and scientist turn in that direction. The rhythm of love is enacted by a science, understood in the Kantian sense, moulding nature to the laws of mind, confronting nature and bringing it back to contemplation in the mind's focus.

Art provides a more sensuous example. Consider, with Plotinus, two stones: one of them has been sculpted into the form of a human figure; the other is untouched, untransformed. Only the first has been changed by love: by the artist's prehension of what he considered the stone's form— that is, its tendency as mere medium—and by his creating of that form until it coincided with the ideal of beauty as he grasped it in this particular situation. The stone has been torn by form out of nature. This is a brief illustration of the violence of self.

Much more could be said on such points. But these slight examples must do here for evidence that the rhythms of self turn about the axis of love. The self, in its rhythms, brings the ideal as well as the natural world to its focus, like a glass drawing scattered rays of the sun. One pitfall threatens such action: the acquisitive self may return with a deceptive and tenuous aura from its excursions into the world beyond. We may wonder to what extent the sculptor finds, in the stone he carves, an embodiment of an aesthetic ideal which has nothing to do with the nature of the stone; and to what extent the natural scientist, in moulding nature to the laws of his mind, is not simply thinking about his own mind. The answer depends on the kind of adjustment which self is presumed to have to what is beyond it. By its nature, this kind of decision is impossible: anyone who could make it would have to occupy a position outside self.

It follows that uncertainty haunts the self in its efforts to increase, to be more: self may be fettered to its own mysterious nature. This possibility holds for language, too, as well as for the whole self of which the exercise of language is part.

The linguistic act has the same rhythm as other expressions of the self and as the self. I mean the rhythm of encounter, essentializing, and reality-making which I have called "love." The rhythm of naming is a paradigm for the rhythms of the self and can be picked up in echo all through that self.

iii

We come to the nature and context of naming in the love-rhythm of the entire self. I want both to move forward in the line of this discussion and back toward the first remarks on naming. So I turn to the question of fiction and its relation to the act of naming and will discuss literature and myth, the two chief fictional creations which emerge from naming.

As fictions, literature and myth illustrate naming's developed "natural" work. They appear early in man's name-work, as the first linguistic creations of civilized peoples. Ritual, out of which myth apparently grows, and epic, in which the early heroic spirit of a nation embodies itself, are man's first forms of civilized expression. *Gilgamesh,* the *Bhagavad Gita,* the Homeric epics, are repositories of ritual and of spontaneous poetic feeling. All three epics expressed the nascent self-consciousness of their peoples. Such fiction is still the first or natural language of man. Children still turn first to fairy stories or to television westerns.

In one sense we have prepared ourselves to see naming as a ground for such fiction. In the sense that naming moves away from the named. This tendency of language to become a creation of new reality rather than a model of old, or given, reality is continued in its tendency to become myth and literature. In naming, the Ur-motive of fiction-making appears.

This is not to say that fiction is the "right" use of language—that is another question—but only that fiction is a natural use of language. The question of norms for naming has no place here. It introduces complex issues, as the controversy concerning emotive and referential language—the so-called languages of poetry and science—has shown. In that controversy, to which I. A. Richards gave a decisive modern form, the "rightness" of scientific language was identified with its un-naturalness. Scientific language was looked on as a corrected form of natural language, from which the emotive, non-significant elements had been removed. This position has since been modified by Richards and its other defenders; I only hint that an equation of naturalness with "rightness" in language is not a priori convincing.

There is a more convincing clue to the way naming grounds fiction-making; here, too, the normative question for lan-

guage should be put aside. I said that the self's effort, in
naming, is not mere verbal play but is part of its overall effort
to translate the outer into the human. This situation follows
from the unity of the self. In such unity the expressions of a
core-movement, the self, all bear the character of that movement. Each expression bears the core's character. Thus, the
rhythm of self in naming, though it transacts with only a
fraction of the outer, summons the whole self to the activity.

It follows that, in the natural course of naming, the self's
translations into human reality will bear its own character.
The self is the core of humanity: its translations will reproduce, often obliquely, humanity's inner physiognomy. Schel
ling emphasized this feature of genetic language when he
wrote that mythical figures are "autonomous configurations
of the human spirit." W. M. Urban expressed a similar idea
from a different angle: "The anthropomorphic form is the
only possible way of rendering the anthropic, the only form
which gives intrinsic intelligibility in connection with man."
Outer reality, reality in a secondary sense, is an unknown
language out of which self must translate into its own language.

Schelling's remark suggests the relevance here of mythical
and literary fictions. They are composed of images of self: of
gods, men, and women, and in that obvious sense the characters of fiction are "configurations of the human spirit."
They are natural flowerings from the ground of fiction: the
kinds of translation of the outer which we would expect from
naming. But in a less obvious sense, too, fiction represents
inner human physiognomy. Mythical and literary themes,
longing, heroism, conquest of death, consummation of love,
enact symbolically the themes of life. The imagery of fiction,
often rising in metaphor to ambitious statements about divinity or the order of the cosmos, expresses frankly humanized
angles of vision. Even the least arrangements of syntax reflect
the aural and verbal taste of the fiction-maker: "le style c'est

l'homme." In these senses fiction realizes itself as the most direct reflection of the self, therefore, as a continuation of the humanizing mode of naming.

It may help toward precision to comment, even hurriedly, on two other approaches to the description of fiction-making. Much has been written about the origins of mythical and literary fiction. In this age conscious of universal themes and motifs—from the viewpoints of Freud, Jung, or Frazer—the common nature of all kinds of fiction has quickly been seen. In dream, fairy tale, or heroic epic we are ready to see the work of our collective subconscious or folk-consciousness. The origin of myth has been conclusively traced to ritual: Lord Raglan, in *The Hero,* has supported his claim that myth is "simply a narrative associated with a rite." The work of the Cambridge school, Frazer, Tylor, Harrison, and Cook, was a brilliant groundlaying for Raglan's view. On the other hand Susanne Langer, in a quite different way, has treated the origins not only of myth and literature, but of music and religious rite. In *Philosophy in a New Key* she argues that an autonomous symbol-making faculty is the origin of our religious, mythical, and artistic modes of existence. Both of these positions, the historical and the empirical-philosophical, have had great influence.

I mention this partly to establish a context and partly for contrast. Not because of disagreement, although there is some of that, but to show the distinctness of my notion. I have something different in mind. I am not concerned with the historical origins of fiction, though I would suspect any theory which couldn't be accommodated to reliable theories of that origin. And I am worried by Susanne Langer's disinterested characterization of the symbol-making faculty as an autonomous part of our psychic equipment. I have tried to establish, for naming, a more vital context in self.

A program has been followed which would describe the grounds of fiction and do so from the inside: a program which would present these grounds, that is, as permanent psychic conditions of fiction-making. In this sense I have sidestepped history. I have been equally anxious, though, not to leave fiction-making without a context in the efforts of the self, a context which seems to me more relevant than history to an understanding of the grounds of fiction-making.

It seems to me that the work done by fiction-making, in continuing the humane translation of naming, is a form of knowing. The experiencing of that work can be cognitive. This is not true in the sense that fiction, especially myth, is a substitute physics, an oblique metaphor of physical reality, or that literary fiction is a direct image of life. Nor is it the case that fictions give knowledge about successful social behavior. Rather fictions are a translation of outer reality into a language, the self's, which is intelligible to man. All naming performs that translation; but fiction is par excellence the unreconstructed language of self.

This fictional translation of the outer can be appreciated by reconsidering the elemental contact of self with outer in the making of names. From the outset self tends to draw that outer up into the focus of its own consciousness. That effort is consummated in fiction-making, where the complex *Gestalt* of the self's matured encounter with the outer is given a form and image which the self creates. In the reading of that fictional form—our first and most natural development of naming—we get humane news of the inhumane outer. That news is the kind of knowledge we are best fitted to take in. Yet the mind cannot test the ultimate status of that knowledge.

2

LITERATURE AND KNOWLEDGE

> *Literature is the complete knowledge of man's experience, and by knowledge I mean that unique and formed intelligence of the world of which man alone is capable.*—ALLEN TATE

Knowledge is highly respected because it is considered a way of possessing the truth. Creators with words—it holds for artists in general—have suffered from the implication that they, as literary people, lack knowledge, and that their works do not embody it. They find this accusation serious, and it is. For if literary people and their works do not embody knowledge, if their drawing-up of reality is not a participation in the truth, it seems to follow that their works are lies. Some critics have tried to make the most of this conclusion by confessing that poetry is a lie, yet insisting that it is a noble lie, nobler than truth. But most reflective literary people have hesitated before such a position and have been ultimately unwilling to agree that their works embody no knowledge, possess no truth. I have suggested at least one line of argument against such a charge. Now I want to shift the defense to a different plane.

This time the argument will be more "psychological," less concerned with the placing of literary activity in its metaphysical setting. I wish to consider one of Plato's attacks against literature, then to build a description of literature by

16

which that attack can be countered, and finally—in a brief concluding comment—to suggest a way of describing the kind of knowledge embodied in literature.

In the *Ion* Plato makes his cleverest attack on literature. There he shows Socrates playing with the vain rhapsode, Ion. Socrates wants to show that the poet or, in this case, the reciter of poetry, is an ignoramus, at least to the extent that he is a poet or reciter. To do this Socrates questions Ion, who is fond of reciting Homer and who considers himself an authority on the epic. Socrates asks him how much he knows, or Homer knew, about the various crafts or skills which Homer treats, like fishing, riding, or military strategy. Upon Ion's admitting that a fisher, a charioteer, or a general, respectively would know more about his own trade than Homer would know about it, Socrates inquires whether there is anything about which the poet can be assumed to have the best knowledge. Ion at first says "everything," then admits that he can't think of anything. So Socrates presses the conclusion that poets in general have only a half-way, dilettantish kind of knowledge. At best it is second-hand and second-rate knowledge acquired from the better informed. Presumably Ion, if he had not been so flustered by this attack, might have answered: "But poets know more about the human heart than anyone else." Who knows how Socrates would have handled this? In our century he might say: "A psychiatrist or a priest knows more than a poet about the human heart."

This is a challenging case against literature, and one which deserves the perennial consideration of literary people. How is this challenge to be met? Is it possible to counter the Platonic charge directly, by *proof* that literature deals with, or embodies, important knowledge and truth? It is hard to see how. It is perhaps better to start a stage farther back, with a description of what literature is. I shall do that, and then return to Plato's argument and to a general relation between knowledge and literature.

What is a work of literature? A definition will bring us quickly to the matter. A work of literature is a deeply unified verbal event occurring in a self. By using the noun "event" I emphasize that the literary work happens in time, takes time. Therefore, it has a beginning and an end, and usually a middle, a crucial center. By describing such an event as "deeply unified" I mean that the words which compose it are, in some sense, literally one. But I also mean that those unified words have several levels of meaning. These provide depth. These levels can be described in many ways. One way of dividing them—which gives at least the general idea—is into levels of (1) dictionary meaning; (2) contextual meaning; (3) symbolical meaning; (4) meaning which can be added through interpretation; and (5) inner aural and visual overtones which accompany the literary event. By saying that a work of literature is deeply unified, I mean that most or all of these levels are made one in it. I add, too, that such a work is an event which occurs in the self. I mean to stress its non-physical character.

It will clarify this definition to ask what it excludes, among those things which resemble works of literature. Conversation—all but that of the angels—is excluded. It usually lacks either depth in its unity or unity in its depth. But perhaps no one would propose conversation. The person who *might* propose it could—following up that point from a different angle—still request a more inclusive definition of "a work of literature." He might ask: "What about those material objects, books, in which literature is written down and, above all, preserved? Why exclude them from the definition of a literary work?" I would answer that literature is only accidentally transmitted in books. We don't want to confuse its nature with the means for its preservation and spread. Finally, a third person, concentrating on a different part of the definition, might ask: "Why speak of a literary work as an event, rather than as a sum total of the events which it takes part in, or as some kind of qualitative average of those events? Is a particular work created anew every time it is read?" To this last I answer "yes." Each work of literature *is* created anew every time it is experienced; is, in fact, a new work. There is a resemblance among the many recreations of the same work. But that resemblance is only accidental to each recreation itself. It doesn't affect the newness, the sudden "Happening-in-timeness," of each recreation. A work of literature has a present but no past.

I agree, though, that something is lacking in the definition. It is life: a quality to suggest the vitality of the literary event. Let me color the pale statement that literaure is a deeply unified verbal event taking place in a self.

The unifying of different depths of meaning, and of inner visual and aural overtones, leads such an event to become a new world, sighted from a hitherto unknown peak on the mind's Darien. It is a world with its own space, character, and action. Those three elements of the literary work are not the same as their counterparts in the "real" world, the world "outside," but it still makes sense to refer to the furnishings of the literary world with the familiar words, "space," "character," and "action."

Consider the element of space in literature: the plain before Troy in the *Iliad;* the hollow cave of Dante's *Inferno;* or the endless sea in *Moby Dick.* These settings are vague moods, contributing depth. They are not mappable, and they are imprecise. On the other hand, however, consider a room-interior described in detail by Balzac; or the inside of a trucker's restaurant, made intensely clear by a few lines of Hemingway. Few things the outer eye sees are as "precise" as the quality of these interiors. Here, then, are two different kinds of literary space. Yet there are two characteristics which the grand scene and the precise interior in the experience of literature share. First, they both exist on the tenuous surface of an illusion. They are conjured up like genii from Aladdin's lamp and can disappear in a flash of inattention. They share this quality with most of the dimensions of mood in literature. Second, both these forms of illusory space embody the essence of the feeling appropriate to them, in the "outer" world, and embody it more deeply than grand or precise spaces in that "outer" world. The depth-mood of the plain at Troy is a perfection of the "real" experience of a plain-space. The same holds for the precision-mood of a Balzac living room which is far more precise than most non-literary visions of a living room. Literary space, in short, seems to be "outer" space essentialized, brought, in its distinctive character, into the inner experience of consciousness.

What about the characters around whom a literary event crystallizes? Think of Achilles in the *Iliad,* of Hamlet, or of Anna Karenina. These characters rise as rapidly as "spaces" to the surface of the literary illusion. They take their positions in the mind's geography, but continually wax and wane in prominence. We encounter them, in a sense, as partially developed modes of our own selves. Each character elicits us to a certain point, then leaves us, encouraging the diffusion of our attentions over the dynamism of the whole work. Yet we feel, in the fullest of these characters, a wholeness of "personality" which we seldom find in our friends to whom bodies are attached. "Bodiness," the fact of being incarnate, makes the difference.

The same observations apply to the action which is the unifying principle in literature. Who of us is the vehicle of actions as whole or realized as Achilles' return of Hector's body to Priam in the *Iliad?* Or as convincingly brutal as Raskolnikov's murder of the old woman in *Crime and Punishment?*

It is not that we need ever to have performed or even thought of performing actions similar to those which literature shows realized. The success of literature does not depend on *that* relation to life. In the same way it was not necessary that the plain should suddenly strike us as the ideal of the experience which a particular battlefield in our own lives once formed. Or that the character of Achilles should catch up and unify the half-clear traits of a war-hero friend of ours. The literary realization of life is oblique. Such obliqueness is alchemical, transmuting the very experiences which are its elements. This is a difficult relationship to explain, not only because it is magical, but because we are blinded to its magic by our frequent half-conscious assumption that "lived-life" is a succession of clearly experienced actions, characters, and settings. We often fail to see either the possibility or the need of clarifying daily life. Actually daily life is vague, continuous, phenomenal, playing over the surface of the senses with kaleidoscopic randomness. Life, in its usual state, is minimal consciousness, out of which emerge only half-clarified percep-tions. It is these perceptions, fragmentary feelings drawn from the awareness of different kinds of character, act, or scene, which are synthesized by important literature and turned into new life. Achilles draws together many ragged ends of mood: our mood of admiration for the soldier who went off to war in a fine uniform; our merest feeling of scorn for the sulking child who cried because his toy had been taken away; our surprised feeling of love for some violent and vindictive man who took pity on his enemy. All or some of these feelings, many which are far more obliquely relevant, and the dynamic form of the self which binds them, are roused to a rare common life by Achilles. "He" is typical of the literary char-acter who unifies and focuses the threads of blurred "real" experience. Literary space and action do the same for us, in ways so complicated that the explaining of them would require more attention than can be given here.

These remarks on literary space, character, and action hint at the vitality of the literary work which had been defined as verbal, deeply unified, self-held. But the remarks lead fur-ther, to at least a comment on the world of literature, in which space, character, and action are parts, but which is more than the sum of those component parts. That world is not a refuge from the daily world. It is no idyllic cave dug safely into the protected slopes of the self. But in the world of literature the chaos and blurred focus of daily, encountered character, space, and action are clarified. Even when these parts of the literary world remain imprecise, as certain grand literary landscapes do, they give to the blurred focuses of real life a deep mood and an accessibility, at least, to conscious experience.

With this in mind, we return to the starting point, Plato's criticism of literature. There is the argument of the *Ion* again.

Socrates had asked essentially this: can we gain any knowledge from poetry, or from a poet as poet, which we could not better gain from a specialist—that is, a fisher, charioteer, or a general—who really knows about the particular subject introduced by poetry?

The question is still hard to answer, because the answer depends on the definition of "knowledge." But one thing is immediately clear: the poet's activity differs by nature from that of the people—fishers, generals, or psychiatrists—who exercise special knowledge about special objects. The poet attempts something different, to create a new world. In making that world he *does* embody material which is proper to a specialist's knowing: he considers theological dogma (as in *Paradise Lost*), battle strategy (as in the *Iliad* or *War and Peace*), or medical science (*The Magic Mountain*). But the poet does not embody that material because of its inherent truth or its practical rightness. In fact there would be nothing impossible about a good modern epic which assumed the truth of Babylonian astronomy and was based on it, or a good sanatorium-novel which was full of outmoded medical thought. Literature is not obligated to reproduce "correct" or up-to-date knowledge, but to clarify and deepen the real, un-rationalized world which we experience as a confusion of intermingled space, action, and character; in short, literature is to clarify and deepen daily, lived life. The elements of specialist knowledge get into literature only because they are part of the setting or mood of experienced life. But the same can be said for stupidity and unreason: they are part of that same setting and have equal rights to the hospitality of literature. Bad logic is often a most effective source of good dialogue in a novel.

It follows that Socrates' attack on Ion is only half-valid. True, the poet, and his poetry, do not possess the knowledge which we expect of the specialists, an account of whose activities or trades finds its way into poetry. But the poet is not concerned with, or responsible for, that kind of knowledge. He is not in competition with the general, the doctor, or the fisher, and the fact that the poet does not have their kind of knowledge does not prove that literature embodies no unique knowledge.

In fact it seems to follow that literature *does* embody unique knowledge, in one sense of that word. The work of literature has been characterized as a unified, mind-held world in which the component space, character, and action participate with a depth and wholeness which we seldom find in them as objects of ordinary experience. It can already be seen, in this definition, that literature springs from a unique cognitive power and embodies its own kind of knowledge.

After reading the *Iliad* one's experience of war is simply more open and perceptive. It is not that the situation of the *Iliad* will be repeated in similar form, or characters like Achilles or Hector reappear. Literature does not, like science, aim chiefly at establishing predictability. Universal types, of course, do recur in literature, serving as the bases of the literary "universal." But they are not in the center of literature's effort to clarify daily life. One's experience will be more open and perceptive after reading the *Iliad*, because the mood and implications of war will have been clarified, deepened, through the experience of a magically simulated war-situation. Similarly the painful experience of doubting can never be equally brute after a reading of *Hamlet*. We do not need to sympathize with Hamlet or identify ourselves with him. But in experiencing the mood of his existence we enrich our awareness of the mood and ambience of doubt. And we carry this enrichment back to daily life in the dynamic structure of our selves.

This kind of artificial clarification and deepening of life through the dynamic experience of literature is the way in which literature gives knowledge about daily life. I mean that literature gives us the power to understand that life better. "The power to understand" something is "knowledge" of something. What else can knowledge be, even about the natural world or about God, except the power to understand them? Yet literary knowledge *is* unique. This kind of literary power could *not* be given to us by priest or psychiatrist, because they could only tell us about life, not present a clarified model of it to us for experiencing.

3

HEIDEGGER AND THE GODS OF POETRY

Es fehlen heilige Namen....
—HÖLDERLIN

If literature can accurately be said to capture and embody knowledge, it follows that it embodies "truth" or objective reality. The capacity of poetry to capture reality, in the highest sense, has in our day been most forcefully asserted by Martin Heidegger.

His aesthetics, which amounts to a theory of poetry, is of the greatest importance as an effort to argue the fulness of poetry. The argument is a dominant concern of his recent thought, and shows how much its author had profited from the experiences with Being which he had already dramatized in *Sein und Zeit* (1927). Like all his thought, Heidegger's aesthetics is intended for the initiate and demands participation. It rewards a good reading, though, with latent power for new experiences of art.

Heidegger claims that poetry, or art, is something *real*. This is the basic assertion of his aesthetics, if the word "real" is taken seriously. It is no mild assertion, for it distinguishes Heidegger from all unthorough apologists for poetry. The defense of poetry as an interpretation, or merely an imitation, of nature, is familiar. It is a commonplace in the history of aesthetics. It confirms us in our "reasonable" feeling that art

25

is *somehow* real and *somehow* an illusion. Yet it does not oblige us to take our aesthetic experience seriously; as seriously, for example, as we have always been exhorted to take our inward "religious" awareness. This defense takes no step toward launching us further into reality through art.

Characteristically, Heidegger explains the reality of art in several ways. In his essay "Hölderlin und das Wesen der Dichtung" (1936) he grounds the reality of art in that of language. Man, he says, is the creature who must bear witness to what he is. "What man is" means "what structure of reality he is." Man must bear witness to "his belonging to the earth." The character of this belonging is that man is both a beneficiary and a learner. He holds these poles of his situation in poise through "inwardliness" and testifies to his belonging to this inwardliness through the creating of a world. This testimony to his belonging to the earth, to all things in their totality, occurs as history, that is, as the consciousness of a temporal context, the making of a realm of time around one. But history only comes into being through language. Language is the raw material of the newly created world. It provides definiteness and character for that world. It goes without saying, therefore, that language is real; that it is the condition of our existence as historical beings.

It follows that the creation of language is a serious and responsible event. Just as this event creates our historical existence, so it creates the possibility of danger, that is, of the threatening of Being by existing beings. Through speech the openness of Being is laid out before man, and in that openness he may go astray, risking the loss of Being. That loss was not possible prior to speech, for the possibility of the winning of Being did not exist; but now that loss is a permanent threat. In humbler terms, since speech is called on to create a world, it may be called to account, like God himself, for the quality of the world it creates. This danger for man is created by speech. So is the related danger of speaking "unessential words," words which may appear to seek Being but actually only mask it. Speaking well, that is speaking in consonance with Being, is never easy, and must be guaranteed continually in the doing, without reference to *apparent* qualities.

Poets are especially fit for such doing. Poetry is the embodiment par excellence of an effort to move into the openness of Being: for poetry, at its best, "founds that which is lasting." This is a paradoxical assertion. One might suppose that "the lasting" could not be founded or brought into being. By definition we are accustomed to think of the lasting as that which exists in complete independence from us. This paradox takes us far into Heidegger's thought. Already in *Sein und Zeit* he made it clear that he believes Being, or the lasting, must be revealed in order to exist. One way to understand—if not necessarily to agree with—this point is to see that Being has no past. It is only the revealed. "What remains will *therefore* never be drawn from the transitory." It is the job of the poet, particularly, to "found" the lasting over and over again. Poetry, consequently, is "real" in the highest sense, and the poet is the priest of the real.

The word "priest" is nearly appropriate here. Heidegger writes: "The poet names the gods and names all things in that which they are." We hear much about the gods in Heidegger, particularly in his discussions of Hölderlin's poetry, and although we are never given a definition of "gods," through context we are made to feel their "presence" as the highest expressions of Being. They are lasting; yet they are attainable only by the naming of things "in that which they are." It is not, Heidegger points out, that an arbitrary name must be provided for what is, but that an "essential word" must be found to open up the reality, the Being, of each thing. At such a finding the gods reveal themselves at once: "The presence of the gods and the appearance of the world are not merely a consequence of the actualization of language, they are contemporaneous with it." The finding is not mere luck for the poet, and his song is not a random song in the dark, for "the gods can acquire a name only by addressing and, as it were, claiming us. The word which names the gods is always a response to such a claim."

The poet, who names the reality in which the gods are, projects himself farther into reality than do other men. In fact, he becomes a demigod, one who experiences Being and returns as a revealer of Being to other men. This is hard work. For not only are true poetry and the true poet rare, but in our time true poets must endure the temporary absence of the gods. The poet, as poet, exists between the "vanished gods" and the "coming gods." Heidegger admires Hölderlin's dramatization of this situation of the poet, in his own poetry, and elaborately analyzes that aspect of Hölderlin. In Heidegger's deep studies, *Erlaüterungen zu Hölderlins Dichtung* (1937), he discusses the poet's need to wait, to remain faithful to the memory of Being, then to protect and preserve the Being he finds. He congregates much of the conceptual point of Hölderlin when he writes:

So for the poet's care there is only one possibility: without fear of the appearance of godlessness he must remain near the failure of the god, and wait long enough in the prepared proximity of the failure, until out of the proximity of the failing god the initial word is granted, which names the High One.

As the expression "initial word" suggests, Heidegger supposes that the poet *as poet* is always beginning, always existing out from the origin of his self.

The "point" at which the gods appear in poetry—rather, in art in general—is more precisely plotted in "Der Ursprung des Kunstwerkes" (1936). This long essay inquires what is the Being in art. Heidegger considers the joining and strife of world and earth the structure of Being in art, thus the "point" at which the gods may appear. Earth, here, means the unformed, inert component which the artist "uses" for his work, and which is called medium. World means the "world" of attitudes and traditions, in short, the "spiritual" ambience which the work radiates. Heidegger describes this art-world in a Greek temple. Before the temple was built, there had been only a potential: carrying plateau, a blue sky, and the sea in the distance. After the temple is built, the nature surrounding it is defined, made accessible. The people who use the temple are given a distinct vision of the reality around it and a defining center for their own experience. "Through its presence the temple gives things their first form, and it gives men their first view of themselves." Being a work of art means presenting such a world. But "the work as work is in its essence producing." The work lets the earth step forth in all its massiveness, and "the producing of the earth fulfills the work, in which it returns itself into the earth." The world in the artwork is continually drawing the medium forth, while the medium pulls the world back into it. This is the strife of world and earth which is for Heidegger the structure of Being in art. A mere thing or a tool distinguishes itself from artworks by its lack of poised strife. The mere thing is all earth without radiance, Heidegger believes. The tool has a world; it springs from creative effort to form a medium. But that is an effort to use (in effect to misuse) the medium, not to deploy it in its own character. Only the artistic work lives from a tensile, but mutually respecting, relation of world and earth.

In these terms Heidegger speaks of the truth of the artwork. In his essay "Von Wesen der Wahrheit" (1943) he defends the idea of truth as revelation rather than as conformity of "thought to thing." To put it briefly, he holds that truth is the unveiling of Being and exists only in our creative relationship to Being. The truth of art is also revelatory: "Thus it is a question, in the work, not of the reproduction of an individual existence, which happens to be present, but much rather of the general essence of things." The artist must release all things in their totality into the openness of Being. This he does by bringing into play the strife of world and earth. That

strife is a model of the "general essence of things," a new
world. But it must be created. That creation is an establishment. "The essence of poetry is the establishment of the
truth." For, as Heidegger has said before, the poets "found"
what lasts. Whether Heidegger calls that "lasting," "gods," or
"truth," he means one thing: that Being which lies under each
existing thing and needs only to be revealed.

The chief problem for Heidegger's philosophy of human
existence, a problem with which he struggled as early as *Sein
und Zeit,* lay in its denial of norms for, and outside of, that
nomena ($\lambda\acute{\epsilon}\gamma\epsilon\iota\nu$ $\tau\grave{\alpha}$ $\phi\alpha\iota\nu\acute{o}\mu\epsilon\nu\alpha$) of human existence and to chart
existence. In that book, Heidegger tried to read the phe-
the realms of authentic and inauthentic existence. Yet he tried
to make that charting without reference to god or nature,
standards outside existence in terms of which measurement
and comparison with existence would be possible. He tried to
explain how existence authenticates itself in the process of
existing: such self-authentication consisted in accurate self-
discovery through acts of the self. For Heidegger denied that
man has even a definable essence which he can discover and
employ as a norm: he may only bring his essence into play
through act. In Heidegger's terms, existence precedes essence.
Heidegger would go no further toward prescribing even an
inner norm than to repeat Goethe's paradoxical exhortation:
"become what you are."

It is no wonder, then, that this problem reappears in Heidegger's aesthetics. It is an important problem and deserves
attention here; the inspection of it is central to any commen-
tary on Heidegger's aesthetics. It will be clear that he has, in
that area of his thought, treated the question of norms with
great circumspection.

He seems to be tempted, but no more than that, to consider
poetry a self-certifying, self-sufficient activity. From the outset,
he sees language as a bridge cast off into the open, detached
from what it was originally supposed to "name." We feel that

language may be left to wander through reality like a ship without a rudder or a pilot. We may look, for example, at the discussion of Hölderlin's "Heimkunft" in *Erlaüterungen zu Hölderlins Dichtung*. There the poet describes the joyfulness of the Bodensee as he crossed it on his return to Swabia. He describes the lake itself as joyful. Heidegger appreciates and "defends" this description; he asks in effect how long we will assume that things and our feelings or descriptions of things are different, that a lake is something other than what we name it or what we "feel" in its presence. Why do we talk so piously of the "reality" of some un-named body of water, as yet unknown to man, which we now call the Bodensee? Language creates reality. Language creates a world. By such creation man testifies to his own existence.

Such testimony is a self-sufficient act. Yet Heidegger is not content with that formulation, any more than he has ever been content with an extreme of "subjectivism." He will not entirely agree that poetry certifies itself, bears its own credentials. For speech has a direction. At least the highest speech, poetry, is an effort to carry on a dialogue with the gods. And since the poet is commissioned to bring back news of the gods to other men, we judge that those gods are a universal good and an end of speech. But not only does poetry, as speech, work *out* from its own center in a direction. For, as has been seen, "the gods can acquire a name only by addressing and, as it were, claiming us. The word which names the gods is always a response to such a claim." The poet's direction through speech is not only not fortuitous, but is guided "upwards" by the gods.

I have also observed that this is not the only concession made by Heidegger to the danger of considering linguistic creativity a self-authenticating adventure into the openness of Being. Artistic truth, the "point" where the gods enter art, is, in Heidegger's ontology, another more-than-artistic structure which serves as a kind of norm for art. Yet are we to consider this primarily a norm "inside" or "outside" of art? What kind of standard for art is being considered? It may help in grasping this particular norm if we look at another example from Heidegger's thought. In his description of the structure of existence, in *Sein und Zeit*, he spoke of inauthentic and authentic existence. Authentic existence was in accordance with the nature of one's self, as Heidegger described that nature. Inauthentic existence was basically a loss of self. It may seem that Heidegger confronts us with a "normal" judgment here, in the traditional sense of the word. Yet he emphatically rejects that way of envisaging his problem. Moral judgments rely on the application to human existence of concepts which are presumed to have an "absolute" existence independent of human existence, of concepts like "goodness" or "justice." For Heidegger such conceptual externality disqualifies moral judgments from any relevance to the radical existential context of each existence, its attribute of being-in-the-world. That being so, he limits the norm of authenticity to the "inside of" Being. His notion of art-truth is a norm for art only in the sense that authenticity is a norm for existence. The artist and his work must strive to reach a tense poise of medium (earth) and world, in which the essence of things will be realized. This act of realizing, as we have seen, is simply the bringing into clarity and definiteness of the network of "relations" which are founded by the artwork. As an act it occurs totally "within" the work of art, or in the artist's creation of it. The art-truth thereby produced is a quality which can at least be *thought* apart from the purely aesthetic existence of the work. But it is a norm which cannot be *applied* from outside. It is an element in the internal creative or appreciative experiencing of the work.

In his notions of gods and art-truth, Heidegger tries to treat the problem of aesthetic norms without violating his conviction that art is a "world of its own." He sets out directions, or paths, through the open, and yet preserves for the latter its "open" quality. Even Heidegger's idea of the claim which the gods make—a "word from beyond" to the extent that Heidegger ever hears one—is a minor confinement of the openness of Being. For the gods exist only by the grace of speech, and therefore can be external to it only paradoxically.

The truth of art revealing the ground of Being may bring many kinds of more-than-human figures into relief. In Greece these figures were deep expressions, virtually definitions, of experience of the phenomenal, or the "appearing" world. It is said and repeated that Apollo was the sun god; Athena, the goddess of wisdom; Ares, the god of war. There is some truth in this manner of speaking. Sun, wisdom, and war were preoccupying features, or themes, of phenomenal existence to the Greeks. They were—in most different senses—basic building elements of every psyche's constitution. The pantheon of believed-in gods—from Homer on these were the Olympians—provided a model of the basic experiences of life. This model could be kinetic, embodied in stories interweaving the gods, and could conform to the dynamism of experience. Homer set the pattern for such a presentation. Or the individual gods could be made the object of the worshipper's attention. The sculptors, with their individual, standing figures, established this tradition of piety. In either case man was projecting in his own image figures to which he voluntarily attributed perfections, eternal life, perfect beauty, which he knew he lacked. And most relevant, here, man was speaking through the artist, which, in Greece, generally meant through the poet. He was relying on art-truth—in something like Heidegger's sense—to illuminate the ground of Being.

This Greek experience is one kind of revelation of the "gods" through art, in Heidegger's sense. Can we then expect that *our* poets will utter divinity in the Greek, or the Norse, or the Slavic way? By the nature of the case we cannot know. Heidegger insists on this. But we can guess and with Heidegger's own authority. If our poets are again to make gods out of the truth of art, they will emerge from the inwardly constitution of our experience of life. They, the gods, will be Being as it is illuminated for us, in our present existential context.

A poet must reach the gods *through* poetry: Heidegger tells us this. But as the poet works experientially into his verse he will find that nature, as distinct in the broadest sense from what man has made, will be the matrix of the gods. Here, I believe, we moderns have had our own literary experience. We have seen attempts to create technical divinities, gods of the machine, or mythologies of utopian society. But these efforts have on the whole been unsuccessful, because they have not arisen from intimately human preoccupations. Mechanism and society cling to the peripheries of the self's consciousness. Only the natural context from which we have emerged and to which we return can elicit our deepest affinities to it through all our powers of knowledge. When we are able again to name the essence of things artistically, our naming will illuminate natural deities. They will be its gods.

Many directions are possible to us, and they are worth at least brief envisaging. In following the bent of our deepest form of knowing we may recommence with a form of the Greek vision: art's truth-making may again enable sky, sea, sun, and moon to burst into named divinity. If so, we shall be less imitating the Greeks than rejoining them in a deep form of self-expression. The forces that join and maneuver natural phenomena may find holy names: energy, love, transcendence may in some form become the new names. Or, in terms of "natural" experiences, we may find a new vision. For us that finding may take a long time, but for Being—as Heidegger reminds us—it will not be a long time. Being has only a present and no past.

In some such terms I read the continuing intention of Heidegger's notion of gods as poetic norms. His own thought recurs frequently to the Hellenic model, and yet is deeply rooted in the "present." Perhaps the Greek mythological vision reoccurs simply because we cannot conceive another. Newness, that which yet comes, is by definition unpredictable. Prediction will not help on that which yet comes, either. It seems the solution cannot be that easy. For, as Heidegger has said, only the poet's patient standing near to the roots of his being will help. In the meantime, though, prophesy at least keeps our minds on the importance of inner norms for poetry. It reminds us that art-truth, even as the revelation which Heidegger calls it, is not complete. It is the light in which the gods, those forms of existence which have most concerned us, can reappear. And it is thus, I think, the key to the infinite gravity of art as an undertaking.

Part II

4

PSYCHOANALYSIS AND THE STUDY OF ANCIENT GREEK LITERATURE

> *Psychoanalysis buries its undertakers.*

Discussions of the cognitive value of poetry are as various as the varieties of poetically useable truth. I have begun with three such discussions. In each the activity of high literature was found to essentialize, condense, or distill "ordinary" human experience, whether of the outer or the inner world. In one case the world seemed to be "drawn-up" into literature; in another, "clarified" by it; in the last, the case of Heidegger, held in its pregnant potentiality by literature. By choosing these so different lines of argument—though they converge at one point—I intended to exhibit the question of literature and knowledge in some of its complexity.

It seems of particular interest, now, to consider what is going on in the making of such high literature. In a sense that was the issue earlier, when it was asked how the named found its way into the name, literary order into the chaos of vague experience, or the truth-value of "gods" into the art-world. But in all those cases the "how" was being discussed in a thoroughly general sense. The perspective was "philosophical." In the first and third essays the language of discussion was

39

"metaphysical," while in the second it was broadly "psychological." Even in the second essay there was no hint of "depth psychology." There was a philosophical discussion of mental process. I turn now to the deeper psychic processes by which the material for literature—outer world, inner world—is translated *into* literature. As far as possible, I will enter the domain of "science," though it is still the "science of mind." And because this inquiry is unmanageably general, I will turn to one particular body of ancient Greek literature, and ask depth psychology to comment on the making of that literature.

At present three broadly different ways of analysis back into Greek literature recommend themselves, the first two largely—perhaps unfortunately—speculative, the last more specific, and until now much more tried. First there is analysis of culture, as Freud conceived it in some of the writings of his last twenty years. Here he was not interested in literature, except at most as an expression of art, which was in turn the expression of a compensation of exemplary importance for the making of culture. But Freud was greatly concerned with the question of what activity art is in the economy of human spirit. The second question, one proposed by Adrian Stokes in a fine, neglected book, inquires into the kind of projection which literary or other art is; into the way and extent that such self-expression detaches itself from its maker. This question differs from the larger cultural issue. Here we are concerned with the kind of existence created into specific works, in the earlier question with the price paid by spirit for the very existence of those works. The last question approaches the themes and larger organizations of language—specific symbols, images—which are operative in the production of ancient literary works. I like here to think of studies like Ernest Jones's *Hamlet and Oedipus* or of still—so far as I know—uncreated studies which will take image material like that in W. B. Stanford's *Greek Metaphor,* and submit it to analysis. For this an analytically-oriented Caroline Spurgeon would be needed. We would get a *Sophocles' Imagery and What It Tells Us* from the Freudian (or Jungian, or Adlerian) standpoint. However, for most such purposes the Freudian approach proves the most valuable. I will at any rate emphasize it here, and in doing so must apologize for repeating some well-known material.

Freud's analysis of culture first operates most generally, as a reconsideration of civilization's differences from the precivilized human state. In his later works he suggested a theory—simply his own myth—of the origin of religion from a sense of guilt for the killing of a primal father. He deduced civilization too from activities of the superego; especially from man's willingness to impose the principles of the tribe or culture on its individual members. Artistic activity, being a hallmark of civilization, is hereby brought into the argument; art, like the civilization which promotes it, springs from the sublimation of animal, id-filled impulses, which are themselves residues of the precivilized state. Culture in general is made possible for man by his relegation of the primitive, which is always threatening, to the prison of the unconscious. The precariousness of the cultural achievement has never been better dramatized than in the late Freud, and an awareness of his argument is indispensable to a student of such an *early,* highly civilized culture as the Greek.

Freud also suggests specific applications of the intimate relation between culture and the primitive nature underlying it. We may, for instance, consider the human tendency toward *Grausamkeit* (brutality, cruelty). Culture is purchased at the price of great suppression or sublimation of such drives; they must be repressed, rechanneled, allowed to escape into more refined expressions of aggression than would be natural to "primitive man." Yet such drives are inevitable components of human nature, and will in some form find their way out into culture. Homeric epic lets them out, in its fashion: in the Laestrygonian attack on Odysseus' men; Odysseus' blinding of Cyclops; Odysseus' killing of the servant girls; the Doloneia, where Odysseus and Diomedes slaughter the sleeping Trojans; Achilles' mistreatment of Hector's body. The epic handles brutality, as it does its entire world, without comment, approval, or judgment; editorial comment must be provided by us. How near do we find Homeric brutality to a "healthy" precultural brutality in which cruelty is functional, serves practical purposes, is related to real ends (like the terrifying of enemies, or the testing of new members of a community)? How much explicit neurosis enters in connection with the Homeric expression of brutality?

Functional primitive brutality, springing from untamed id, is not far in the background of most of these literary events. The Laestrygonian attack, the killing of the handmaidens, and the Doloneia are highly verbalized accounts of what must in very early society have been socially effectual, and not uncommon, brutalities. The meaning of "very early" is not of much importance here, particularly as we have little exact idea of the date of composition of the Homeric poems. It is safe to imagine that in Homer's people's tradition the memory of Minoan or early Mycenaean brutalities, vengeances, exemplary punishments, must have been fresh. I see no reason to deny the romantic view that Homer himself could translate those memories directly into literary detail, making in art at least an obliquely faithful replica of important social conventions. But the blinding of Cyclops and the defiling of Hector's body make us think further.

These examples show the reworking of primitive aggression into a form of specifically cultural interest; in which that aggression can, in the medium of language, be transmitted broadly to a large audience, who can then take vicarious pleasure in the verbalized drama. Neither Odysseus' treatment of Cyclops nor Achilles' of Hector is demanded by the literary situation of their epic.

Inevitably the blinding of Cyclops by a burning pole is a folklore motif; it has its precedents. But it is not adapted passively by Homer; he makes it yield its refined brutality. In adapting it Homer provides pleasure by indulging both himself and us in a sadistic feast of a sort forbidden normally in society, at least unless clothed in garments of self-righteousness. The narrative is detailed, far beyond the point required to free Odysseus for further wandering. The heating of the pole, the arrangement of the mechanism, the drunkening of Cyclops, and then . . . the delicious turning of the singeing instrument in the great, single, soft eye. It is part of Homeric genius that the whole episode, apart from the question of pace, is functional, needed for the freeing of the hero. In the *Niebelungenlied* there is cruelty for its own sake, not furthering or affecting the epic's progress. In Homer all the cruelty is at once sadistic in itself and related to the necessities of the story.

Achilles' mistreatment of Hector's body is equally perverse. It is already clear, in the first book of the *Iliad*, that Achilles is divinely neurotic. The cruelty of such a touchy powerful man will, if released by personal affront, free primitive aggression. The death of Patroklos unlocks the passion which issues; Achilles weeps and rolls on the dust in his lover's arms. There follows the frightful scene in which Hector's body is dragged around the walls of Troy. Then Achilles tries to let the body rot outside his tent. Such sadistic violence has no parallel in Greek literature. Oddly, though, it seems less a rage against the bonds of culture than do such outpourings in Euripides and Herondas.

It is the old question of Euripides' *Bacchae*. We are not to suppose that the weight of sympathy there aligns itself with Dionysus. Pentheus is a prig and inflexible, by general agreement; but he is honest and responsible to what he knows, the safeties of the polis. Yet Dionysus is destined to victory. By this time, in the development of Greek culture and of the Greeks' awareness of their culture, an attitude such as Pentheus' seems completely inadequate. This is now, as we know, a culture of the highest refinement, in which the awareness of repression has developed proportionately to the sense of cultural achievement. The two senses proceed together. The more complex the culture, the more precarious its relation to nature; this precariousness is felt from within. It is not to be found in Homer, who in certain instances can take great simple interest in the return of primitive feelings, say in the form of sadism. That sadism is masterfully handled, from the literary standpoint; but Homer does not seem to feel, in letting it out, that he is releasing forces of such violence that the existence of society depends on their incarceration. By the time of Euripides, and in him, awareness has come to that. Dionysus is a particular form of the id, which has become so menacing to the polis-sheltered civilization that its breakthrough can be both disastrous, because dissolving all the newly achieved bonds of society, and beautiful, because offering the distant, primal, and oceanic again.

Much in Euripides offers the same awareness. Heracles' heroic humanity, in the play of his name, is volcanically perched over a madness which wrecks the conscious mind. Medea, from the land of the magical, the subliminal, travels with the man of reason to the civilized land of the ego. There she is double-crossed by the rationalizations of a disintegrated personality. Her indoctrination to civilized responses has been too brief, and she goes wild from within. The tension between unsubduable passion and learned shame tears Phaedra apart. The *Orestes* is a drama of the overcivilized, in which too long suppressed libidinous drive bursts apart the last scions of a great family. (A kind of Attic *The Sound and the Fury*.)

In Euripides, Freud's conceptual point about the price of

culture, and its dangerous relation to nature, is *the* implicitly embodied argument. In Homer, this argument had been far more secondary. Culture had not yet removed itself to a polar distance from nature; it had not forced itself to become so aware of what it was. In the second century Herondas we meet a still more evolved stage. Changes could as well have been shown in Aristophanes' *Ecclesiazusae* or *Thesmophoriazusae,* or in Theocritus. I am simply going to the end of the development.

Mime one is a good introduction. Gyllis, the bawd, tries to talk Metriche, a younger lady whose husband is off to Egypt, into forming a sexual liaison with a second man. He is reputedly wild for Metriche, and Gyllis provides the full details, the sweat of his passion. The description steams with innuendo. It is all kept fantasy and frustration, however, by Metriche's flat refusal. The projection of pander's psychology is left hanging, and the aroused libido of the mime remains unfastened and central. The Euripidean pander-nurse, as in *Hippolytus,* sees her point through. But Herondas is not interested even in catastrophic consummations. Incompleteness fosters the effect of loose neurotic desire with which he wants to fill his work.

Mimes three and five are sadistic and invite strange comparisons with Homer. As in mime one, there is a close, even intimate relation among the dramatis personae. In the third, a mother stands by to supervise a schoolmaster who is whipping her retrograde son and his worthless pupil. Each "knows" the other; there is an incestuous spiritual inter-involvement among the three. In the fifth mime a lady confronts her slave, of whom she is agonizingly jealous; he has been sleeping with another woman. She decides to have him whipped, sends him off to the whipping post in custody of another slave, at the last minute calls him back for a preliminary tattooing, then is talked out of the whole enterprise by her daughter, who has been present all the time. There is here a

remarkable intimacy of tone, a close interrelation, and mu-
tual interaction among the fellow characters of these little
pieces. Epic sadism was, by contrast, strangely impersonal.
Achilles seemed to be enacting, against the hated Hector,
almost a rite of vengeance, a pattern of activity which for all
its violence was strangely formal. And of course the Cyclops
had no personal identity to Odysseus. The great single eye
might as well have been on a jellyfish.

The climate of sadism has here changed in a far more
important way, however; Herondas marks a new stage in
Greek literature, one which will reach perfection only in
Petronius' elaborate indecencies. In Herondas neurosis is
literarily exploited for the interest which it provides. It is
no longer a question, as in Homer, of a genuine story in the
context of which sick moods naturally arise and pass into the
whole. This much might, though, be simply a question of
the totally different genre in which Herondas creates. However in him it is not even a question of the completion of the
scenes in which neurotic atmosphere is conjured. The first
mime sets the type. The lady-pimp conjures up desire, then
nothing is done even to pursue her proposition. The desire-
talk is all that is left. The third mime ends with the distraught
mother running home to get leg-irons "so that as he skips
here with his feet together the Lady Muses, whom he has
hated so, may witness his disgrace." The fifth ends with the
infuriated mistress retracting her punishment at the last
moment. All this is pure frustration. There is no need to
press the contrast between Herondas and Homer on the
matter; Homer has no interest in neurosis for its own sake.
Yet he is a mind far too civilized and far too complete to
sidestep portrayal of neurosis in his panorama of human
existence.

These are sketches for a (primarily Freudian) history of
the return of the repressed in Greek literature. On a larger
scale they represent the kind of psychoanalytic study which

might be applied to any literature, in order to show what is going on in its making.

There are vast possibilities latent in such "technical" re-readings of Greek (or any other) literature. At first it might seem that the course of such a literary history would follow the expected pattern: that from the earliest (Homer) to the final (Herondas) stages of ancient Greek culture there was evidence of fairly steadily increasing repression, thus of increasingly more sublimated, and in that sense refined, artistic expression. But my few examples, I think, show the far greater complexity of the entire inquiry. In a sense Homer and Herondas are not, in the examples considered here, exemplifying the same question as Euripides. He is putting the general issue about the very possibility of repressing the id, and suggesting the frightful consequences of its sudden and violent release. Homer and Herondas are showing forms of one pathology, sado-masochism, which becomes the content of the suddenly breaking-out id. But Homer and Herondas could both be read in terms of the more general topic: eros (the pursuit of Helen) might be taken as the single source of violence in Homer, and passion, in both Homeric epics, as the sole motivator—whether of Odysseus' delays on the way home, or of the entire Trojan expedition; while some of Herondas' hyper-civilized mimes could be taken to illustrate the prurience underlying normal, or ostensibly normal, social relationships. Euripides, on the other hand, could be read for more sado-masochism: we could inspect the relation of Electra to Orestes in the *Electra;* of Clytemnestra to Agamemnon in the *Iphigeneia at Aulis;* or of Medea to Jason. In any case it would take some work even to co-ordinate our arguments concerning Homer-Herondas and Euripides, respectively.

There would then be the question of historical correspondences, which would reveal themselves at the widest intervals, say between Homer and Herondas, and which

might be lacking at close temporal intervals, as between
Euripides on the one hand, and Aeschylus and Sophocles on
the other; the latter pair would reveal relatively little of interest to the present question. Unexpected results, here,
would be multiplied by the addition of other, clamoringly
relevant, texts: Anacreon, Sappho, and Archilochus; the late
Aristophanes; Menander; the *Greek Anthology.* I can imagine, in this way, an involved history of repression and aesthetic expression in Greek literature. It would help to bring
an entire literature up for fresh considerations. It would at
the most be a method applicable to other literatures and even
to questions of literature in general.

It would be a more familiar kind of inquiry, at that, than
the one proposed by Adrian Stokes in his *Greek Culture and
the Ego,* an examination of the modes of projection of experience in literature. Supporting himself on Melanie Klein,
and so ultimately on Freud, he analyzes the particular capacity of the classical Greeks to project realized and separated
images of themselves into religious, artistic, and philosophic
forms. "Images of themselves," in this sense, are to be understood either as the literal images, which we find in anthropomorphic religion and drama, or more loosely as representa-
tions of the "ego-figure." The latter might be architectural
forms (the Parthenon), lyric poems, or even philosophical discourse (like the dialectic of One and Many in pre-
Socratic thought). What matters, there, is that the projection
should reflect the integrated and realized harmony of the self.
What matters in both cases is something difficult to state: that
the projected form should have inner integrity and autonomy,
great "thereness": that it should preserve its "separatedness"
from its creator while at the same time, obliquely, embodying
the integratedness of the creator.

The groundwork of Stokes' argument is his analysis of
the Greek self. He claims that the Greeks were skillful at
bringing up children and at fostering their projective powers.

He discusses this skill in twentieth-century terms. The habit of separatedness sets in early, at the second year when, according to Melanie Klein, the infant faces a crisis. He has been growing increasingly aware of the evils of the world: of the retractibility of the breast and then of the other good, i.e., breast-like, things in his world. With this growing awareness of "evil" grows a sense of the otherness, the out-thereness, of the world beyond self. During the crisis of the second year the child tests his ability to accept the existence of a world beyond. If he cannot accept it, he plants in himself the seeds of neurosis. If he passes the test, he is at least on his way toward a mature acceptance of the objective existence of the objective world, as well as toward a mature strengthening of his own self (or ego) for what *it* is. This kind of maturity, Stokes believes, is prerequisite to any ability at projecting a real art or thought world, in the image of the self but separated from it. Quite apart from the strength of this underlying psychoanalytic argument, an ambitious cultural analysis is here being developed from psychoanalytic principles.

It is worthwhile suggesting some specific applications of this entire analysis. It could be pursued into the religious creations of Homer's epics, the literary ones of Sophocles, or into the sculpture of the fifth century. It could also be applied to some other literature than Greek. I will deal here only with a few examples.

The gods of Homer, we often say, are the Olympians at their most representative. We mean that the distanced but sensible humanity of the Greeks themselves seems to have put itself most completely into those superego projections: into Zeus, Poseidon, or Athena. We immediately notice, in those figures, that closeness to humanity which seemed so objectionable to later Greek critics like Xenophanes and Plato; while to many early Church Fathers the anthropos-like traits of Greek gods were direct proofs of Greek godlessness. There was an accurate insight in these criticisms, as far as a theistic viewpoint was concerned. What they missed, though, was the firm and highly distanced separation of those gods from their makers and worshippers. The great Olympians in Homer are uncannily human, brimming with mortality; yet at the same time they are wholly realized in a world of their own. *This* kind of separation from the mortal, in fact, was quite unknown to the later theistic critics of Homer's gods. The Christian god, though often believed beyond all attribute and sensible approach, was continually felt and experienced in the intimacy of the soul: he was if nothing else a god who confused himself with man.

Such religious projection in Homer is, according to Stokes, characteristic of the instinctive classical Greek strategy; it reappears in the best literature and sculpture. The latter case is perhaps clearer, and certainly easier to appreciate, in connection with the verbal portrayal of gods. As those gods make their ways into sculpture, they preserve their Homeric bearing. It is enough to think of the early archaic Athenas, the thunderbolt-bearing Zeus (or Poseidon) from Sunium, the Apollos of the fifth century: that gallery in the midst of which, as Goethe said, *"man fühlt sich in einem bewegtem Naturleben."* The extraordinary experience is, once again, of figures living within themselves, realized in thereness which is not the hereness of the maker, yet which is at the same time profoundly human, fully accessible to the ordinary human equipment of the beholder. No later parallels will come to mind, I think, before Michelangelo; and few after him.

Finally, there is the literary situation. The entire literary world created by Sophocles suggests itself. Where Aeschylus perhaps leans away from the human, and Euripides in toward it, Sophocles keeps the strategic projection, of interest to Stokes. It is seen in whole thematic conceptions: the story of the Theban house, with its totality of human responses and inevitable human tragedies, yet its almost ritual distance from usual human experience; the tale of Philoctetes, full of compassion and agony, yet realized at a level so fundamentally human that it must seem, in the partial vision of the individual human, to be "beyond" individual experience, distant in depth. Individual characters illustrate more convincingly, and what must be said, in this connection, can be managed in terms of Oedipus. It is a commonplace that he is all of us; his generative power of representing man has resulted in endless interpretations: making him into the eternally honest rationalist; the eternally deluded mortal who is himself the flaw that he proudly seeks in others, but who has the courage to admit this; the eternal humanist, answering "man" to the Sphinx, then affirming the dignity of man, even in agony, so completely that the universe finally accepts his transcendence. Yet he is, by common consent, none of us. His existence is within himself, even when he acts, and within it he seems as totally self-contained as an inscrutable archaic Apollo. There is no way for us to break into the magic circle of his organic existence.

There is great danger of laboring such points and of degenerating into impressionism. Stokes avoids the danger entirely by basing his observations about the distance of projection in Greek literature, art, and religion on a technical theory to which he can fasten his impressions. That theory is psychoanalytical, boldly reducing achievements of the classical mind to the crisis of the second year. I don't insist that this kind of reduction is accurate; all psychoanalytic reduction, it seems to me, is somewhat crude, because it says too simply that what I experience is not really what I seem to experience, but is something else. But such a theory, I am certain, is far more than just stimulating. It strikes toward the truth, which is that the kind of world a man projects, in any of his self-expressions, will depend on what kind of man he is; that what kind of man he is will depend on what kind of infant he was; and that what kind of infant he was involves matters of the most intimate relation to parents and to the pattern of infantile sexuality. It is unfortunately difficult to determine when Sophocles began toilet training; but such knowledge would probably help us to understand Sophocles' literary achievement.

A third application of psychoanalysis is the most familiar, the most tried, and at present the most respectable: I mean the explicit analysis of literary motifs, or themes, or archetypes as they are found in literary texts. In English we know this approach from Ernest Jones's *Hamlet and Oedipus,* Maud Bodkin's *Archetypal Patterns in Poetry,* and by now from a variety of articles. Wellek and Warren, in *The Theory of Literature,* look on *this* psychological approach as the only genuinely literary one. They are most doubtful about the contributions of any other approach to the understanding of literature.

The tracing and analyzing of myths in literature would lend itself to indefinite extension into the study of Greek literature. The little that Jones and Wertham write on this topic suggests unexpected perspectives and profitable lines of new research. It is only an accident of the Freudian bias of these writers that the Oedipus complex has chiefly drawn them; certainly they provide awareness, between the lines of the Oedipus drama in Sophocles and of the Oedipus drama in all Greek literature, for which we are grateful. Hidden motivations, presumably hidden also for the authors of those works, are made clear, and words are given more dimensional meaning. Some work has been done to extend such analyses to the Oresteia theme; an Orestes complex has been christened, by Wertham, for cases of suppressed and finally "realized" matricidal tendencies. Yet in that direction *this* kind of analysis merges with the first kind studied here, for which I gave examples of the return of the repressed id in sadism.

Connected with such myth-analysis is the study of literary archetypes, an analysis of literary works largely in terms of applied *Jungian* psychology; although Maud Bodkin, who offers the only extensive example of such work, does not by any means restrict herself to that discipleship. Here one can study recurrent literary patterns, such as that of the theme of death and rebirth, of the cycle of the seasons, or of the conflict between the generations; literary patterns which Jung viewed as embodiments of primal, inherited mental patterns. Or personality types can be studied in literature: the *ewig weibliche:* the dependent son on whom extraordinary burdens are placed (Orestes, Telemachus), and who grows through bearing them; the hero who descends to the dead (Heracles, Aeneas). The metaphysical status of these archetypes remains quite uncertain. Unless we can still maintain, as Freud and Jung did, Lamarck's theory of inherited mental acquisitions, it is impossible to attribute these archetypes to inheritance. And Lamarck's theory is very doubtful. Yet there is a more-than-individual status to literary archetypes. Even if they are transmitted only by and in society, through education, it must at least be remembered that such themes are part of a society which man makes as well as being made by.

The three ways of analysis back into Greek literature are three ways into literature in general. I am concerned, at this point, with what is going on in literature, and I suspect that the three "ways" discussed here all take us further toward *that* answer than any of the rather metaphysical ways discussed first. Those first perspectives of analysis were not intended, after all, to reveal the intimacies of the literary process; only to put the intimacies in an abstractly universal context. The psychoanalytical approach is still universalizing; still, obviously, preoccupied with *classes* of mental operation. But it is concerned with classes whose representative states are tangibly present to the individual. It remains to see whether there may be an even deeper—though there is hardly a more tangible—analysis of what goes on in the making of literature.

5

PALAMAS, LORCA, AND THE QUESTION OF TROPES IN LITERATURE

> *A gypsy-woman nursed him; that is why he has wings.*—SERBIAN SONG

i

Both Kostes Palamas, the father of modern Greek poetry, and García Lorca wrote about gypsies. Lorca's *Romancero Gitano* (1924–27) is well known in America. Palamas' much longer and much more ambitious *The Twelve Words of the Gypsy* (1900) is still little known, though it deserves ranking with the major efforts of nineteenth-century epic.

The two works have much in common, and I shall begin with their themes, which are noticeably comparable; as is something fundamental in the way they handle their themes. In discussing the question of "handling" here, I will still be involved with the psychic processes operative in the making of the two gypsy poems. It will be a question of what the figure of the gypsy means, and of why and how gypsydom drew these two poets similarly. By asking ourselves on this level what it is that we can compare between the *Romancero Gitano* and *The Twelve Words of the Gypsy*, we will raise a theoretical question of great interest for the study of litera-

54

ture. How far are we, in the comparing of works, limited to comparisons of language and theme? Do we—can we?—compare the psychic processes behind works? Of what use is it to think that we can compare something "deeper," between works of literature, than shapes of language? And finally, a more nearly ultimate question: is there *something,* shared by works of literature, which exists at a level deeper than that accessible to analysis of the sort considered in the preceding chapter?

Lorca's sequence of poems is all sense. Image melts into image in a drunken, pouring kaleidoscope of words. Preciosa runs, followed by the "hot sword" (*espada caliente*) of the wind; while around her the "flutes of shadow sing/ and the snow is a soothing gong" (*Cantan las flautas de umbria/ y el liso gong de la nieve*). Juan Antonio de Montilla falls dead down the slope; "his body is full of lilies,/ a pomegranate in his brain" (*su cuerpo lleno de lirios/ y una granada en las sienes*). The "church is growling like a bear, belly up" (*La iglesia gruñe a lo lejos / como un oso panza arriba*). At every turn we are forced to this level of immediate experience.

At the same time we are storing larger awarenesses of the "gypsy world." Song by song we realize more fully the gypsies' passion, pride, sensuousness, innocence, and final fatedness in an alien world. Passion (in "la Casada Infiel") leads the gypsy man and woman down to the river at night, but pride keeps him, the narrator, from "loving the woman," because she had deceived him into thinking her unmarried (*"teniendo marido/ me dijo que era mozuela/ cuando la llevaba al rio"*). The sensuousness of the gypsies' way of experience is everywhere: the gypsy nun's "heart of herbs and sugar,/ Of spice and sweet,/ is broken" (*"se quiebra su corazon/ de azucar y yerbaluisa"*); or St. Michael (a Granada saint)

...rich in lace
In the alcove of his tower,

Shows his beautiful thighs
Ringed in the lanterns' light.

Yet the repressive modern world closes in and destroys such people. Antoñio Camborio is killed by four envious cousins, members of the Guardia Civil. Or the surreal reveries of the gypsy girl, in *Romance Sonambulo*, are broken when the "Drunken Civil Guards/ Hammer on the door."

Deeper than any of these portrayed aspects of gypsy life is love of freedom, and deeper even than that is the "sense of freedom" which pervades these poems. "Love of freedom" ascribes too clear an intention to the gypsies; it is rather that they live in a world which is still in many ways pre-repressive; vastly more so, say, than the world of "primitive man," which we now understand as a mesh of confining tabus. The *casada infiel* and the narrator of the poem make love with a whole delight, which is the free releasing of them both until the end of the poem, when the *casada's* lie is learned. In the first poem, *Romance de la Luna, Luna,* the child has astonishing, pre-scientific sensitivity to moonlight and the presences latent in it; he is free in the pure magic of the universe. Little Antoñio Camborio, although captured and killed by the Guardia Civil, remains free in the sense that he will not succumb, but fights the system to the end. Through all these accounts flows a larger mood of freedom, contributed by the poet, who in writing about those free spirits bathes their world in a primal sea of free human awareness.

Lorca's *Romancero* is brief and dense. Palamas' gypsy work is loose and epic, divided into twelve wide-ranging cantos—the "words" of the title. It unfolds around a central figure, the Gypsy, and his wanderings—both physical, toward Constantinople (the City), and spiritual (through his encounter with the main issues of his epoch and of man in it). The gypsy is first seen drifting on his mule, toward the City; he is an unbindable free being, wandering through a land-

scape which is essentially the geography of his own spirit. Into
that freedom enters the necessity of a livelihood: he becomes
a bronze-worker, a flute-player, a builder; then the lover of a
partridge-breasted gypsy woman. Finally he nears the City.
We feel all life streaming there, along with the rider. At last

>...the triple golden gates
>and the brazen portals screeched
>a screeching as though a man were groaning,
>and without a human touch,
>magic and double-width
>they opened wide themselves.

After this point we are more intimately *in*. The splendor
sensed becomes an intensity lived on all sides, drawing in the
Gypsy and driving from him extraordinary projections of experience. He encounters a procession of scholars marching to
the harbor; they are about to sail off to the west, saving the
accumulated manuscript wisdom of antiquity. The Gypsy
joins them in thought. He sums up the value of their books
and chants with them the hymn to all spirit-things that trans-
cend. At the same time, though, he stresses his own supremacy.
This time he is sublimely flippant:

>I fear no Turk
>no thefts of slavery's clutchings catch me
>nor does your Greece amaze me,
>nor have I been drunk
>with incense from an outworn cult,
>from any worship.
>And if I find some papyrus scroll
>I burn it just to get
>some heat or light...

His felt superiority pervades the next "word," where Chris-
tians are seen burning the books of the Byzantine Neo-Pla-

tonists, those thinkers who were at the time trying to revive
"ancient" paganism. The two groups, present at dawn in the
City, confront each other while the Gypsy listens; then he
counters them both, speaking for Nature against both revealed religion and paganism. He has been with a band of
free mountain Thracians, from whom he learned that wisdom is the purity of freedom:

> In their existence the milk of health
> and the blood of sacrifice were reconciled. . . .

These men are the Gypsy's heroes. The force of their race
around him is dramatized in the seventh word. A great
Gypsy-Festival is being held in the Meadow of Kakkava, just
outside the City. International Gypsydom is present: colorful,
turbid; scholars and fools and seducers. They are pageanted
in an enormous spate of words. An emissary of the Emperor
enters, offering the gypsies a new homeland in Sparta. The
Gypsy refuses, for his people, in a hymn to harsh freedom,
which builds on his earlier passion for Nature.

As "prophet," in word eight, he sees the evidence of the
city's corruption, and the proof of his own thought's strength.
The Emperor is found watching races in the Hippodrome.
Around him, like the jewels of his imagination, sit his courti-
ers. Below him are the people. Suddenly a messenger brings
news that the Turks are at the city gates. To arms! The Emperor says no, raising his head slightly in refusal. The games
must continue. The pleasures of the city must not be inter-
rupted. Let the Turks do what they will. The Gypsy, who
has been present, prophesies death and eventual resurrection.
Then he becomes again a chanter of mysterious élans. In word
nine he finds a violin. Into it he pours his soul, finding with
astonishment that the entire power of his nature is released,
that what is essentially music in him emerges in a dithyrambic
praise of existing. We have almost earned the Gypsy of word
eleven, the canto of the Tearless One, whose legend becomes

an exaggerated parable of the entire epic. That story, in which
Palamas expresses some of his understanding of Nietzsche, is
in its way terrifying. The Tearless One, transmuted Gypsy,
appears as a grim folk hero.

> He had a father, had
> a mother, only child;
> and he was like the stars
> in the tempest of a night.
>
> Teachers they found for him
> and led him to all places
> and knowledge flamed in him
> supreme jewel of his mind.
>
> And where others feel
> a heart that pounds
> he felt transcendent scorn
> the savage mood of beasts.

He takes all his parents can offer him, and finally sells them
into slavery. Ruthless self-will drives him to unlimited cruelty.
Then he rides, at the King's command, until he meets the
Laughless One, a beautiful woman as cruel as he. He breaks
even her obsidian spirit. This final triumph is instructive;
the Gypsy is (and should be) hard, strong, relentless:

> From his being and his drive
> he will sow his traces everywhere,
> the traces of his passing;
> and bit by bit his joy will spread—
> the hard, the strong, the tearless joy—
> where life is slavery and indolence.

Here we reach almost the end of the poem. There follow a
final "word" and a postscript. In the twelfth "word" Nature
welcomes the Gypsy into her bosom. His spirit is called back
to that powerful simplicity which it had loved. But it is a

soft, diminished "word." While in the postscript, addressed
by the poet to an unnamed woman, we have only an oblique-
maudlin allusion to the whole matter of Fall. The Gypsy's
hardness seems half-forgotten.

As a whole, the poem coheres and compels. The blending
of the Gypsy with the gypsies with the world of the City is
achieved with large synthetic imagination. Many individual
scenes build the power: the first coming of the Gypsy; his
efforts as lover and sculptor; the old men carrying ancient
texts abroad; the Festival of Kakkava; the Gypsy's rejection of
a Homeland for his race; the Emperor's indifference to the
Turks; the Gypsy's prophetic speech; the legend of the Tearless One. Within himself the Gypsy bears meanings which
Palamas fully masters and incarnates. Freedom is the marrow
of all those meanings.

ii

What about the "psychic processes" involved in the making
of the two gypsy-works? How far can we go toward comparison in that direction?

From the biographical standpoint we can see for some distance. We see it "making sense," in both mens' lives, that they
wrote gypsy-poems of this sort. Lorca was brought up near the
old entrenched troglodyte-gypsy colony of Granada, scenes of
which must have impressed him from earliest childhood. He
saw the freedom and passion of these people; as well as their
tragic vulnerability to social hostilities, hostilities which have
always pursued the gypsies. Growing awareness of these people and their customs fostered, and became clearer through,
kindred traits in Lorca himself. In all his writing he valued
independence, a sense of human freedom which he described
and incarnated so well that he was put to death for it. He
was at the same time, and in a totally personal way, sensuous
and innocent: his letters, and the body of his written work,
overflow with these traits. Quite apart from poetry, and the

"gypsies" that Lorca "creates" in his poetry, the man Lorca had deep and obvious personal affiliation with the Granada gypsies. Complete understanding of his making of gypsy-poems is only possible in this life-setting.

With Palamas the biographical relation is more subterranean and oblique. We have here to think of a quiet man, born in the provinces (Missolonghi) when Greece was barely finding itself as a modern nation; coming to Athens, which was very much the big city; trying a hand at politics, but soon finding himself inescapably a poet and *littérateur,* in which capacity he early settled into, and stayed in, a sinecure, permanent secretary of the University of Athens. A quiet passion for the "other," the limitless, the totally free, hard, and virile ran through this existence, perhaps making its placidity endurable. The gypsies, still today seen in Athens, and more in the Greek countryside, were far more common in both places fifty years ago: their first European home had been Greece, and the Balkans were still the most congenial part of the continent for them. These figures became central symbols of Palamas' private myth of the "other." The quiet academician was translating, but not transmuting, the gypsy beartamers who crossed the National Gardens; for the beartamers entered his poetry directly.

As might be expected, the real experience of gypsies and gypsydom had excellent organic reasons for entering the poetry of Palamas and Lorca. The "reasons" are in each case unique, functions of everything distinctive and needing in the two men. Grounds of comparison, at *this* point, are entirely lacking. But there are other "reasons" for gypsy-creativity, reasons equally organic, which are much more nearly common to the two men. I think of the general kind of activity operative in each of these poets, as he chose and projected the image of gypsydom into poetry.

Palamas and Lorca admired above all the freedom of gypsies: they show this by capturing such spirit of freedom in patterns of imagery and larger verbal-kinetic shapes, which are the essence and power of their best poetry. That central "meaning" of gypsydom in the two poets must be distinguished from the various *different* meanings which gypsy-life assumed for them. For Lorca gypsy-life is passionate and sensuous; brilliant color and primitive enthusiasms are the raw-matter of freedom. For Palamas, too, these passions are central to the meaning of gypsy-existence. The Festival of Kakkava, where international gypsy-culture dances for three days, boils with Ur-human energies. The partridge-breasted gypsy is an incarnate eros attributable to *all* gypsy-women. But the center and drama of Palamas' projection is the gypsy of the title, in whom freedom is converted constantly into a conception; as, characteristically, in the canto of the Tearless One, for whom freedom is refusal to be meshed in the bonds of human sentiment. Palamas' version of Nietz-schean freedom is read into this gypsy.

An awareness of freedom, in some single sense, is providing the main energy of both these poems, and is being channelled into the verbal conduit of gypsies and their culture. I believe we see, at *this* level of activity, similar psychic processes going on in the making of both gypsy poems. It is worth digressing here to translate the activity of both writers into other terms, which will make the context of their psychological relationship clearer.

iii

In his later work Freud turned to general social questions in which he began to view the topic of repression from a less uniquely sexual angle than he had earlier applied. He erected the hypothesis (in *Totem und Tabu*) of a primal killing by which a band of brothers originally shook off the yoke of their repressive father, sharing his women and pleasures among themselves; but then, in a reaction of deep guilt for the deed, established the same repression over *their* offspring. This repression was then inherited throughout the generations which construct society, and became a formative factor in the mind of man in society. Finally it became *the* operative condition for the making of civilization. A sense of primal guilt, and of the dangers of liberation from this guilt, were to become central ingredients of the civilized mind and to take their place in all its operations.

Barbarism from within, the renewed tendency to re-enact the Oedipal drama, permanently threatens this psychic balance. There is a compulsion back toward what, in the social definition, must be considered the primal guilty act. Whenever, in individual cases, the Oedipus complex is not adequately worked through, the progress of society is slightly impeded. But inadequate working through and consequent aggression is not the only threat. There is a permanent "danger" from the radical desire for freedom from the "working through," for escape from the profound constraints of civilization. Many members of society want to *elude* the problem. Freud did not pay particular attention to *this* escape-response, this desire which becomes natural in man, to step entirely outside the guilt-inspired repression of society. He remained more concerned with the aggressiveness which is stored up during the working-through of the Oedipus situation, and with what he considered the sense of fulfillment accompanying a satisfactory working-through. But Freud has established a complete context for the understanding of the desire for escape, for freedom, which is subsequently seen to have its roots in the original soil of the human situation.

He thus provided one kind of language for discussing such artistic projections as we find in Palamas' and Lorca's gypsy poems. I believe it is a useful language. It does not offer to put us inside the "psychic process" of authors (such as Palamas and Lorca), though we know from Freud's studies of Michelangelo and Leonardo how far his analyses could lead into the genesis of art. What Freud offers here is more general in application than close psychoanalytic studies of single authors. But it enables us to understand, in some depth, how the choice and projections of the figure of the gypsy and gypsydom could, for both Palamas and Lorca, be part of a larger, and more significant, human trope of escape into freedom.

iv

Perhaps this explanatory notion seems too rarified and general to promise much for concrete analysis. Can we come down to cases?

In the examples given above it appeared that the psychological backgrounds to literary works may be unique and *uncomparable*. There is little to say by way of comparing Lorca's with Palamas' *private* reasons for writing gypsy-poems. In fact the more we knew of each man's personal development—of his childhood experiences, his sexual encounters or sublimations, his particular compromises with reality—the less we would feel able to compare. It is conceivable that there might, *within* these two different histories of development, be a deep tendency, a common "trope"—as I should like to call it—generated by the deepest human concerns; a trope toward freedom, in the present case.

Such a trope, I think, would stand in relation to unique psychological histories rather as human nature does to specific men: their "nature" is the joining factor, their "specificness" the separating factor. The trope would be not even as concrete as a "psychological fact"; it would exist only as a kind of culminating, "ideal" tendency among such facts, yet as a persistent and operative factor in human experience. Its communality among many separate men would make it a peculiarly expedient object of literary study.

The human situation out of which such a trope would emerge is roughly that described by Freud; the drama of man's effort to accommodate (or not to accommodate) himself to culture, thus to the most influential shaping force which impinges on natural existence. We might expect a number of significant tropes to emerge from that situation.

Common sense proposes the varieties, which are widely applicable to literary study. We can imagine tropes in which the curve of projection is freedom: movements of escape. These, I believe, we see in the gypsy-work of Lorca and Palamas, work which is marked by very deep longings to be free of the "problem." Then there are tropes in which the movement is toward "mature acceptance" of basic human repression; literary projections, often in modern works associated with a heroic realism, a hard-headed and conscious "good faith" toward oneself. Other tropes incarnate the feeling of "guilt"; single works or whole bodies of work by a single author, pervaded by thorough acquiescence in the psychic status quo; acceptance of the primal repression, perhaps as a good, perhaps only as a necessity. Finally, although there is no exhausting real examples here, there would be tropes in which the movement of spirit was characterized by "radical innocence." In literary expressions of this movement we would find heavy accent on characters—for this would be a literary-biographical matter entirely—who were simply unable to understand, or find themselves in, the primal social situation. They were not rebelling their way into freedom; they simply never accepted the necessity from which freedom would be wanted.

Examples come to mind, supporting these commonsense categories. The turning toward freedom has been seen in Lorca and Palamas; it was the starting point. As I said, the expression of this trope is given different qualities in the two men's work. But the direction is the same in both. We also find it central, say, in the *Odyssey*, or in Shelley's *Hellas*. In each of these poems—and I note in passing a bond between poetry and freedom—the entire movement is toward freedom. Freedom is not their subject matter, but the curve of activity which they are. Yet in neither Homer nor Shelley is the fundamental longing translating itself as immediately as in the gypsy-poems. Homer's projection of Odysseus is too circumscribed by the question of return, ultimately too social, to be taken as direct expression of the primal condition. In *Hellas*, freedom is both the explicit content and the generative mood behind it; though here, I think, we see all the difficulties of making such a distinction. In the following chapter I will apply the distinction more closely to the *Odyssey*.

Tropes toward mature acceptance seem to be premised on an "awareness of the problem." They are most obvious in cultures with a capacity for inculcating self-awareness in their (literary) members. To find this trope, too, the distinction between underlying curve of projection and actual thematic material must be closely observed. *Oedipus Rex* and the *Divine Comedy* are tropes of this kind. Oedipus is the criminal who only discovers his guilt after a relentless search; by getting at this theme from within, and in powerfully generic terms, Sophocles makes Oedipus live for us as a non-abstract Everyman. Then Oedipus' acceptance of his criminality seems to stand for a universal power of acceptance of guilt. Dante is much less evidently instructive, and embeds his vision deep in implication. By arranging the possibilities of human nature in ruthless totality, and making the observation of this display the theme of his work, he initiates the reader into the whole reality of being man. He does not ask acceptance of this reality, but assumes it with such eloquence that we decide to assume it with him.

Guilt tropes must be distinguished from those of "mature acceptance"; but it would be pure pedantry to press distinctions here, unless they offer themselves naturally. I think of certain works in the Christian tradition as marked by guilt, probably because that tradition has sponsored feelings of basic human guiltiness (which from the Freudian position would appear not as feeling but as accurate presumptions of the true situation). Contemporary fiction like Greene's *The Heart of the Matter,* or Mauriac's *Le Noeud de Vipères,* is based not on a mature acceptance of guiltiness, a "growing into acceptance," but on profound interest, and even fascination, with a state of affairs accepted as centrally human. The trope is soaked in guilt here.

The spiritual movement of radical innocence, finally, would also embody "awareness of the problem," for we should hardly expect to find literary works of merit which proclaimed freedom from the prison of the mortal condition, without being founded on a learned understanding of that imprisonment. I think we must turn to the familiar figures of Roquentin (in *La Nausée*) or Meursault (in *L'Étranger*), for examples, and view the books which embody them as projections of at least the imagination of total innocence. For Meursault the law, an embodiment of *the* human arrangement designed to perpetuate the sense of guilt, is incomprehensible; in a deep sense he cannot be tried, because he doesn't know what it means to be tried. For Roquentin the social myth, and with it at least the customarily imposed ideas of guilt, are hateful, if not meaningless. He is not radically innocent of their meanings, like Meursault, but lives in a state of such basic sense-awareness that he, too, constantly dissolves the banalities of society, and its repressive organization of man, into nothingness. He refuses to grant their existence.

v

The comparison of Lorca with Palamas led to a conclusion: that a preoccupation with freedom was central in those men's gypsy poems; that concern with freedom grew from a psychic stratum, in each man, deeper than that whose interplacements compose the structure of ordinary individual psychological history. I drew on Freud for a description of this realm, or stratum; although I—for one—am uncomfortable with the notion of "realm," which implies a static condition rather than the dynamic process so conspicuous in any coming-into-being of psyche. (Hence the tendency to substitute "situation" or "condition" for "realm.") In an effort to open out that situation, and to make it potentially useable for literary study, I suggested four distinct and common tropes of expression, central to a number of major literary works.

This approach should be distinguished from that of Maud Bodkin, discussed in the last chapter. Under the influence, though not the thumb, of Jung, Miss Bodkin's *Archetypal Patterns in Poetry* examines major literary patterns. As mentioned, she is concerned with the persistent use, in great literature, of themes like that of heaven and hell, of *das ewig weibliche,* or of the pattern of death and rebirth; major human preoccupations which impose themselves, with a regularity attributed by Jung to inherited attitudes, almost ritually onto the greatest literature.

I have also agreed to the usefulness of such a study in the analysis of literature. There is no doubt that these patterns and themes recur persistently, as Miss Bodkin claims. The study of them and of their literary appearance is interesting in the way that the study of folklore motifs is interesting: it is not an aesthetic but a classificatory—and at most an "interpretative"—study. Its most serious drawback, I think, is not that it does not provide aesthetic explanations—it is after all chiefly an analytic weapon—but that it is of very uncertain general speculative worth. This limitation may change. But at present we don't know *why* archetypes and patterns are so prevalent in literature; we don't know *what* to explain in terms of them, or what to explain them in terms of. They are just there, and very much there. They don't fit in.

What I have called fundamental tropes are less "there" than archetypes. At least until more thought has been given to the nature of the fundamental psychic stratum, until we refine greatly on the four categories suggested here and learn to distinguish genuine trope from merely thematic material, we will be unable to feel confident of wide trope-discoveries.

As I have described the trope, it is a general and pronounced projection, evident and deep where it appears, but hard to find and analyze in borderline appearances.

But leaving aside such difficulties for the moment, it is worth stressing (and in one part re-stressing) the value of at least something like this meta-psychological study of literary works. Such study strikes for a level of generation which is deeper even than the "unconscious" psychic history of the individual, with its uniqueness. I have not explained how the underlying psychic situation of the individual is related to the person's concrete history. Simply to say that the former situation is "deeper" is of little psychoanalytical interest, when what is wanted, in the present case, is a dramatization of the interweavings of *original* tendencies with secondary responses and directions of action. But even sidestepping that problem we can still see that, and how, the study of the meta-psychological proves useful where archetype study was useless.

The condition in which these tropes inhere takes its place, in being, at the point where man enters culture; the primal psychic situation is that unremitting drama, in every civilized individual's interior, by which he establishes himself as a cultural being, by which he establishes himself, for instance, as a being who might create literature, that inturned reflection onto the human situation. The meta-psychological state, therefore, is the condition for the possibility of making literature, so that in that condition, quite naturally, lie the sources of certain projectional curves—into freedom, into innocence, into inward acceptance of the cultural condition—which are later to be the deepest distinguishing marks of kinds of literature.

The linking of certain deep and essential traits of literature—certain formative tropes—to the author's primal psychological character is possible; above all it shows the speculative relevance of a meta-psychological critique. In terms of

that critique we can do something toward explaining literature and its roots in the original soil of the human situation.
We win one insight into the relationship between art and
life and another into the relationship between civilization and
barbarism.

6

ODYSSEUS THE HERO

> *For I am no more of an age to re-*
> *main at the farmstead, so as to*
> *obey in all things the commands*
> *of an overseer.*—ODYSSEUS (*Od.*,
> XVII, 20–21)

Will the notion of tropes survive a close look? Application to
the *Odyssey* will be a test. By entering into some detail on the
presence of the trope of freedom in that work, I can suggest
the complexity at least of that notion. Much of what could
be said about the remaining tropes will have to be implied
here. I will at the same time be looking ahead to the coming
argument, where it will be a question primarily of the relation between the author's character and the character which
he projects into his work.

It is useful to think of Odysseus as an existentialist hero.
In many ways he embodies the character which that trend
of modern philosophy helps us to admire. (I am thinking of
the positions of Sartre or Heidegger: not those of Christian
existentialists.) Of course generalizations about a school of
philosophy are misleading, particularly when, as in the
present case, important members of the school have denied
its existence. Nonetheless the portrait of a character-type,
whom we may call an existentialist hero, emerges from the
works of many of those authors.

They argue that man must act without divine advice, that

71

he cannot look to any god for assistance with problems of choice. The grounds of choice are lodged in man himself; they lie deep in the willing and self-enclosed individual. From this assertion the argument proceeds to place great emphasis on free choice; for it is just that choice which makes man entirely responsible for himself. Choice, it follows, is the act by which man makes the future into the present: by which man creates the future, and therefore the world, as far as it exists for him. What could be more important? It seems almost a superhuman responsibility; yet the bearing of this burden rests squarely on human shoulders. This is the burden of our freedom, that "dreadful freedom" of which there is so much discussion in existentialism.

There is a second, closely associated tenet of this philosophy. It is that action is the true character of human existence. Man is born and exists only on the threshold of the new. He is constantly crossing new barriers, entering new provinces. Even tradition is simply a mode of movement forward into New Being. To resist action is to resist life, choice, and freedom. Action fulfills self, and man must engage in it fully, even recklessly, in preference to becoming a tool of destiny, the anti-self, the destroyer of choice.

Yet choice and action are not enough. For man to choose and act in the way proper to the human condition, he needs to be conscious of his context in existence, his "existential" context. Man must be aware of the kind of person he is, must be aware of his true nature, for only then can he strive to fulfill that nature. Authentic life leaves us no room for naive misunderstandings of the kind of being we are. Vainglorious self-heroizing is as grave a mistake as underestimation of self. The worst mistake of all is the loss of self in the impersonal, in what Heidegger calls *das Man*. A correct appreciation of our powers and of the sources of our energy is the basis of choice and action proper to us, the basis of real, as distinct from inauthentic, existence.

Now on the basis even of these remarks there emerges a portrait of the existentialist hero in which we see certain Odyssean traits. The existentialist hero takes the responsibility for his own decisions, which he makes without divine advice. He is a relentless chooser, considering that the future of the world, for him, depends on the choices he makes. Consequently he is set on continual action, believing that only in that way can he choose continuously and exist authentically. Authentic existence, for him, is simply the becoming aware, and realization, of his choosing and acting nature. He is self-conscious.

How does Odysseus fit into this picture? I want to follow him hastily through his story; remarking in order on his power of free choice, his self-awareness, and his activeness.

When we first meet him he is on Calypso's island, in his ninth year. He sits on the headland and weeps, looking out across barren sea toward Ithaca. He is sad and passive: the only time we see him so in the *Odyssey*. He seems to have lost his will and to have given in to sweet Calypsoid seductions. He is tightly bound.

At this point Hermes comes to announce the gods' intention, that Odysseus must leave. The announcement gives the needed prick to the waking will-power. It operates, like most of the divine communications with Odysseus in the poem, to awaken or heighten powers which he possesses latently, rather than to transfer power to him from outside. This point is important; on it depends the understanding of Odysseus as a freely choosing agent.

We appreciate the freedom of Odysseus, even when he is guided by the gods, when we contrast him with a hero like Aeneas. Aeneas' destiny is outside of himself and always remains there; Odysseus' destiny is outside of himself, but it is constantly converted into something of his own. In one sense both figures are subordinate to destiny. Jupiter has chosen Aeneas as an instrument of historical destiny; and, in a sense, Zeus and Athena co-operate to sanction a destiny for Odysseus, even though it is loosely prescribed and enforced. But Aeneas, *insignis pietate,* is entirely subordinate to the destiny laid out for him: he is not free, because destiny is more potent than he is. The effect of his leaving Dido is not that the reader admires Aeneas' strength, but that he looks on Aeneas as weaker than fate. Odysseus, on the other hand, is more significant, and poetically far more potent, than the destiny laid out for him. Hermes, Athena, and Zeus help him away from Ogygia; Ino helps him reach Phaeacia; Athena helps him win the battle against the suitors, and so on: but each divine assistance fosters the vitality and purpose of Odysseus as an independent being, and makes him, himself, appear stronger to us. He is more potent than his destiny because his destiny makes him a salient figure persistently in the foreground of the *Odyssey.* This is the way in which Odysseus converts his destiny into something of his own. In this ultimate sense he is a free agent, and his freedom is the source of his existence. Destiny, through divine intervention, only reinforces potencies in his own character. Formally speaking, he may distinguish himself from the existentialist hero by his concourse with gods: but practically speaking his life emerges from the core of his own being, and thus qualifies as free in a distinctively existentialist sense.

This is the sense in which Odysseus remains free in spite of the will of the gods. He welcomes Hermes' announced encouragement to freedom from Calypso. Perhaps *the* decisive point occurs when Calypso tries to persuade Odysseus to stay with her. She offers him immortal life and a steady diet of nectar and ambrosia. With this, of course, she offers her divine body. Odysseus declines, choosing the finite, kinetic world.

Nowhere is the cleft between his, and the divine, manner of existence brought out more poignantly. He could not have lived by a destiny created in heaven. But Calypso longs for lasting union with a mortal: she is allured by the finite. The limitation of the Homeric gods to infiniteness is as compelling as the limitation of the mortal to finiteness. Calypso is a prisoner of divinity. Ontologically speaking, the gods can have only external effect on mortals. And yet Odysseus has a real choice to make in denying Calypso's offer. He might have been turned into something other than mortal if he had accepted.

This is not the only time that he renounces narcotic, freedom-drugging seductions. He proudly recounts his renunciations of Circe and the Lotophagoi. These accounts emerge from the core of a fictional personality. He talks seductively about the seductive Lotophagoi and of the danger of tasting their narcotic fruit. He knows his enemy. Then he drives home his point. A man who tastes the fruit of Lotus-eaters may stay with those unreal, happy figures, and lose the power to return into the reality of his own being.

Circe, who held Odysseus for a year, was a greater threat. She "swinifies" his men; they were anyway far less than heroes, as the eating of Hyperion's cattle had shown. Those men retained human minds but lost human bodies, a peculiarly frustrating way of allowing freedom to be submerged by matter. Only Odysseus, protected by *moly*, could de-charm Circe, a harder job than blinding a Cyclops in his lair. He did this to release his men from choice-drugging, female witchery.

In all three of these encounters, with Calypso, the Lotophagoi, and Circe, Odysseus chooses out of the strong freedom of his own existence; and not, for instance, in the deliberate, morality-fulfilling way of Bunyan's Pilgrim. Odysseus, by the enacting of his own character, makes his choice clear. He *is* his choice. This parallel of Odysseus with the existentialist hero goes much further: for both heroes choose the real, attempt to enact the authentic, as distinct from the false or artificial. In the three Odyssean situations mentioned here, it is the feminine or effete that is rejected. That is not accidental. Odysseus is a man. Existentialism, in its turn, is a masculine cult: from its angle of vision, too, the feminine principle is dangerous, potentially unreal.

The next meaningful encounter with Odysseus occurs among the Phaeacians. I bypass Nausicaa for the contrast of Odysseus with the Phaeacians.

His return to the reality which he had affirmed on Calypso's island could not be immediate. The Phaeacians mediated it. They were a gentle, rich, happy people, living a conflictless existence. Briny Odysseus invaded them, a meteor of reality in their still sky. The contrast is potent. It emerges at its clearest in the games played on the island, in which Odysseus puts the island's strong men to shame in discus throwing. At that point the Phaeacians re-emphasize: their skills are sailing and dancing; gentle sports for gentle people. These sports are far from Odyssean pastimes. The contrast is visually clear too, in the confronting of Odysseus as *Gestalt* with the soft, easy figures of Alcinous, his wife, Nausicaa, and the court in Alcinous' palace. The long description of that palace, both inside and outside, is one of Homer's most ambitious visualizations. It is a static and sumptuous picture: gold and silver dogs in front of the palace, *kouroi* on their stands in the hall, the leaders of the Phaeacians seated at their banquet, the handmaidens sitting and weaving or grinding grain; all this perfect and still. In feeling, the architecture of the scene is massive and still. Odysseus' entrance is disruptive. Nowhere in the poem is his energy and pragmatic manliness more apparent. He is the acting existentialist in a group of gentle epicureans.

We learn him well while he is on Scheria. His narration of his previous journey, the subject of books nine through twelve, is his greatest self-revelation, the clearest evidence of his self-awareness. I think many interpretations of his narrative have obscured the important point that Odysseus is talking to the Phaeacians about himself. Efforts to identify the places he describes, or the folktales he refers to, are not uninteresting. They are simply peripheral to the *Odyssey*. For in the poem the importance of Odysseus' narration is that he is the narrator, and that he is the person whose wandering he is reporting. The places he visits are simply the background or landscape of his own character.

In this sense the narrative to the Phaeacians might be compared to the lying tales which Odysseus tells after his return to Ithaca. It is not that the narrative to the Phaeacians is a lie; the reader sees no great intent to deceive. But it might well be taken as a phantasy, having no relation to external poetic fact in the *Odyssey*. I suggest viewing it as a tale dreamed up for the insular Phaeacians and representing Odysseus' spiritual autobiography. The entire narrative is pervaded by a strangely artistic self-consciousness. Through the narrative Odysseus reveals another of his existentialist traits, his self-awareness.

He brings himself constantly into the foreground of his narrative, and explores his own personality artistically before his audience. Usually he refers to himself ironically. It is never clearer than here that he is no extraverted Beowulf, or conscience-driven Aeneas. We see it in his retelling of the encounter with the Laestrygonians.

Odysseus tells what loathsome and terrifying savages the Laestrygonians were. None of the destruction is softened. He dramatizes the state of panic which seized him and his men as the savages attacked; admitting that he was as worried as the rest; having ordered the ropes of his ship cut so that he and the men of *his* ship, at least, could escape. This is one of several occasions when Odysseus presents himself to the Phaeacians in a less than heroic light, though he always gauges the effect of his story so that he won't go too far. It is interesting to compare him with Aeneas in this matter. In the second and third books of Virgil's epic, Aeneas is much less conscious of his audience than Odysseus, and much less conscious of the self he is introducing to that audience.

Odysseus shows his self-awareness again in his narration of

the meeting with Cyclops. It is another weaving of self-display
with an active story. First Odysseus describes his own master-
ful solution of the threat of Cyclops. He comes to this only
slowly, after the ponderous killer-monster has been characterized, and his slow destructiveness has been verbally enacted.
The horrible dilemma of Odysseus and his men is dramatized.
It takes time and verses. But only then does Odysseus turn to
his witty, brutal triumph, and savor it in the telling. The
telling is dramatic: partly dialogue of Odysseus himself with
Cyclops in which the narrating hero has become almost an
actor reading two parts. These lines of simulated drama are
a masterwork of self-consciousness. So is the *outis*-joke, which
Odysseus introduces after Cyclops has been blinded. Even
subtler is the cold, impersonal way in which Odysseus describes the infernal device for blinding Cyclops and the blinding itself. Dialogue and personae are abandoned here; science
takes over. This change of pace in the narrative seems to be
Odysseus' way of saying: in spite of my humanity, my flexi-
bility, I was essentially an efficient force, a winning power.
Finally—a refinement rare in epic poetry—he makes fun of
the way he taunted Cyclops as he—Odysseus—and his men
sailed away. He speaks of the danger which he, through
gratuitous nastiness, brought on his ship and men, by way of
the boulders which the blinded Cyclops heaved at the taunting, vanishing voice. I know no other epic hero so sophisti-
catedly aware of his own presence in various situations, or so
daringly willing to pose in less than a stock-heroic light.

The same pattern of self-dramatization and self-analysis
shapes the hero's account of the Sirens. He longs boldly to
hear them, is bound to the mast, and takes exquisite delight
during the passing. He heroizes himself, but with the familiar
half-amused irony. The irony grows sharper as he tells how
he begged his men to release him, while his ship was passing
right before the Sirens. He begged by motioning with his eye-
brows. He tells this without judging himself, just as he was

not judging himself when he spoke of taunting the Cyclops. He is just giving himself that inner dimension which makes him a self rather than a mere hero. The examples of *this* Odyssean effort could be indefinitely multiplied. By nature he is a man who knows who he is, the ideal existentialist.

We see Odysseus next after he returns to Ithaca. He is never put to the *real* test until then. The mysterious, timeless boat-passage back to reality resembles a primitive *rite de passage,* sanctifying a change of status. Odysseus is thrown into reality on Ithaca. He must labor to get into his palace again: he must re-apprentice himself to the authentic. It is here that we see him in action.

His greatest material accomplishment on Ithaca is to destroy the suitors in his halls. He performs the killing with brains as much as with weapons and wins against enormous odds. There is no need to discuss his skill in that slaughter. In itself it tells us nothing new about him. It is more to the point to ask why Odysseus keys himself to this enormous accomplishment. This persistent *why* can and should be asked of Odysseus' acts from our first meeting with him. What drives him? The question becomes more demanding in the last books of the poem. Has Homer's Odysseus any romantic affection for Penelope after the passage of twenty years? Homer makes us doubt. And what about Penelope's own attitude, after the canny interrogation to which she has subjected Odysseus? What does she feel? What does Odysseus think she feels? Is it simply the *principle* of the home which draws Odysseus? The home, with its overtones of ease and comfort, seems an insufficient motive for the all-risking return. Odysseus is far from bourgeois; and is anyway destined, as he has learned from Teiresias, to a life of further wandering.

Odysseus simply considers the situation in his halls an affront to his active self and to the heroic way he lives that self. Evil per se does not horrify him. He can be sly, even cruel. But effete feeding on the hard-earned substance of his home outrages and enrages him. The suitors are totally feckless. They lack even the drive to ask Penelope's father for her hand.

Anything is endurable to Odysseus except the contradiction of his active, free nature. He meets many contradictions to that nature: the Lotophagoi, Circe, Calypso. All those forces could be sidestepped, rejected as peripheral to a (verbal) path through life. But the suitors lay on the path through which Odysseus' spiritual journey had to pass. His own undeniable history led straight to the suitors. They were not only unendurable but unavoidable. Existentialist Odysseus could preserve his character ultimately only through action.

It would have been equally self-contradictory, though, for him to settle down after his victory. He could not have grown soft, had more children, become a duped Menelaus or a gabbling Nestor. In the underworld Teiresias tells Odysseus that he is destined to go on wandering, to travel inland until he comes to people who mistake an oar for a winnowing fan. Only death will end his wandering: a death darkly prophesied to come from the sea and among prosperous people. The Teiresian prophecy stamps process, indefiniteness, and continuity on Odysseus' journey; the right touches for an existentialist journey. It is chronologically the last, but ontologically the first, existentialist trait we see in Odysseus; longing for wanderings was in his heart on Calypso's island.

I purposely chose this example of trope-activity. Odysseus carries with him the central projection of the *Odyssey*, is and makes the curve of its being. In a large sense he is an embodiment of the projection of the trope of freedom. This embodiment is far from complete: I have already said, in the previous chapter, that the return of Odysseus is circumscribed by various social considerations, by at least some considerable desire to impress, effect, and react, in terms of his social surroundings. But to a large extent he is free; in fact one of world litera-ture's firmest monuments to freedom. To this extent the *Odyssey* satisfies the suggested description. It is a work marked by the trope of freedom.

In the gypsy-poems of Lorca and Palamas the value of free-dom was a mood bathing language and events. That state—of freedom—could be ascribed to particular individuals: to the Gypsy himself, in the *Twelve Words;* to individual gypsies, in whom love, for instance, guaranteed imperviousness to ex-ternal discipline. There was also vast admiration for freedom in the attitude shown by Lorca toward the individuals whom he was describing as free. The loose, though disciplined, state of his language enforced the assertion; although in another poet it might not have. In another, *strict* language might have done the enforcing.

In the *Odyssey* the case is more complex. Odysseus is not a gypsy, in Palamas' sense, nor is he one of those sensuous, proud individuals who, as Lorca saw, could never be subdued by "the external." Odysseus has a destiny, which pre-exists him although in a sense it only exists when *he* has decided to give it reality. He is presented, in addition, as surrounded by a world of individuals and obstacles which limit his exist-ence. Even the shaping and flavoring of the language in which he exists constrain him. He is incarnated in strict, though rangy hexameters, and often in the familiar verbal formulae which give a hieratic and archaic mood to epic character.

Yet Odysseus is "free"; makes his own destiny, forces others to define themselves in terms of him, and above all exists as gust and tireless protension from one point in reality to another. And because he *is* the central movement of the epic, he enables us to consider the *Odyssey* as the product of a spiritual trope of freedom. That it is not *entirely* this, or that this is still a very *general* way of talking, is clear. But it is a way of talking, and I think it arouses perceptions; for it strikes at a remarkably deep level of productivity in Homer the creator.

I spoke of Homer earlier in connection with "sado-masochism" and "projection" in Adrian Stokes's sense. There I struck below the surface of language and touched mental processes operative in the creation of epic. Are we now striking at that same level, in touching the source of the trope of freedom? I believe that in part we are—though no assertion could be more speculative than this, directed at a figment of being as shadowy and distant as Homer. We are striking toward a disposition, in the author of the *Odyssey*, which would have formed itself contemporarily with those other major experiences—of sexual domination or passivity, of relation to the breast—which formed his sadistic or masochistic, or his projectional, relations to the world. The trope emergent from that crucial early drama would have been a function of the primal relation to the other, person-and-society, to which the first sexual dispositions were responses. The trope of freedom, to the degree it expressed itself in Homer deeply and from the first recesses, would be even closer, though more "generally" close, than his sexual awarenesses, to the first ground of his existence.

Part III

7

ARISTOTLE AND THE QUESTION OF CHARACTER IN LITERATURE

Le style c'est l'homme....
—GEORGE LOUIS, COMTE DE
BUFFON

In the first three essays I surveyed three general ways in which literature might be said to embody truth or—what was about the same—gather and provide knowledge. (It being presumed that the knowledge was "accurate," so true.) Then I turned to the way in which that knowledge or truth "gets into" literature. I was there, to a degree, reconsidering the material of the introductory essays, where literature's capacity to draw in (or await) knowledge proved to be a *way* of embodying knowledge. But in touching on the methods of psychoanalysis, and of what I called the study of tropes, the argument engaged more closely with the question of the *psychological processes* operative in the making of literature. I was considering literature, there, as a projection from psyche, whereas earlier I was still partly concerned with it as a drawing up into psyche, an "introjection." Chapter 1 considered the drawing up of the named, in personal experience, into literary order and clarity. Certainly it was also a question, there, of "projection"; of the self's way of "essentializing" and putting into patterns of order, of the world drawn up into language. Introjection and projection seemed hardly more than the opposed extremes of a single human process. But the emphasis was strongly on the introjective end.

In the present essay I concentrate on the projective question. Perhaps I am here, no *more* than in the last two essays, concerned with what the self can convey into aesthetic language. But now the interest is in the more complete self, in what is conventionally called "character." That, I suppose, is a more comprehensive organization of traits than are even those subliminal dispositions discussed in the preceding section. I am quite unready, at this stage, to locate tropes in the individual character, or to show what part they play in its establishment or activity. But I am at least confident that character, there, is the more general conception and that the inclination to a certain trope is part of the dynamic situation which goes to constructing an individual's character.

In order to approach the question of how character finds itself into literature, specifically how the author's character finds its way into the characters of his work, I shall begin with Aristotle. The *Poetics* introduces the matter deeply and clearly.

Here Aristotle considers the question in connection with tragedy, which he divides into six elements: plot ($\mu\hat{v}\theta os$); character ($\mathring{\eta}\theta os$); expression of thought ($\delta\iota\acute{a}\nu o\iota a$); diction ($\lambda\acute{\epsilon}\xi\iota s$); music ($\mu o\upsilon\sigma\iota\kappa\acute{\eta}$); and spectacle ($\mathring{o}\psi\iota s$). His remarks on plot and character are of great importance because they establish a conception of the nature of literary plot and literary character which has remained common, almost canonical, to this time. Schoolboys still take their place in that Aristotelian tradition when, at the teacher's prompting, they discuss the "plot" and "characters" of a book, and do so with the Aristotelian assumptions: of the total separation of "plot" and "characters," and of the primacy of plot. Yet there is a serious weakness in Aristotle's notion—of plot and character—at least as we have it in the *Poetics*. After I have

stated Aristotle's position I shall return, with counter pro-
posals and a counter theory, to that weakness.

Aristotle considered the plot the most important element
in tragedy. By μῦθος (from which comes our word "myth"),
he meant an imitation of action—that is, of action in the
"real world." Here, as elsewhere in Greek literary criticism,
"imitation" does not mean simply "exact reproduction."
To what extent it may mean something like "symbolic," or
otherwise "oblique," representation, is hard to determine.
It will be enough, for present purposes, to think of "imitation" as exact reproduction with allowance made simply for
the transference—always radically transforming—into another
medium: from life into art. What, then, did Aristotle mean
by "action"? The noun πρᾶξις (action) takes us back to the
verb πράττω (to do). Action meant a "doing" to Aristotle,
rather as poetry (ποίησις) meant to him a "making." Such
a "doing," then, is a time-crossing event, in fact an event
whose nature is closely involved with its temporal status. Such
an event has a personal agent, or vehicle, and transacts with
other persons, or more generally, with the "other." In fact,
the notion of a "transaction" is especially fitting to describe
action, for that notion emphasizes the dialogue-like structure
of action, which always involves its agent with "the world,"
whether of people or of things. Plot, for Aristotle, was the
turning of such action into art.

Character, for Aristotle—and here again we must think
first of character in "life," not in "art"—meant that by which
a person was of a particular sort (ποιός τις) rather than of some
other sort. Put in another way, character is a quality (ποιότης).
Action, on the other hand, is not "qualitative," for Aristotle,
though it may *reveal* character and thus quality. That is,
things that people do may indicate what kind of people they
are, but those actions, according to Aristotle, *are* not the
qualities of the people who perform them. This point is
sufficiently important that it should be put in an additional

form. Aristotle seems to say that whereas one may, in character, have "goodness" or "badness" as qualities, goodness or badness are not possible constituents of actions. Good men and bad men act, but their actions, which are the chief subject of the imitation which is the plot of tragedy, are not themselves good or bad. This distinction is the basis of Aristotle's particular distinction between plot—the imitation of action—and character, in literature. Plot retains, for him, the unqualitative nature of the action which it imitates. We unthinkingly echo this literary distinction when we say, of the character of Oedipus, for instance, that he was irascible, courageous, and honest—that these traits were his qualities—but of the play *Oedipus* that it concerns a man who killed his father, married his mother, and blinded himself in despair, when he discovered his sins; that is, that it concerns a series of doings which are not in themselves qualities or qualitative. It was in just the spirit of this literary distinction—by which character was considered qualitative, thus passive and inert, while plot was dynamic and unqualitative—that Aristotle considered plot more essential than character for tragedy. Indeed, in a rare burst of exaggeration he wrote: "Without action there can be no tragedy, but without characters there can be one."

What, then, is the relation between tragic plot and tragic character for Aristotle? Does he consider them distinct, unconnected parts of tragedy? Surely this is unlikely: we know that Aristotle appreciated the organic wholeness of works of art. Yet in his brief remarks on the parts of tragedy he does not discuss wholeness. In fact he does not make it clear what he considers the relation of plot to character. Here is a chief weakness in his theory. Yet Aristotle anticipated this objection. (He may well have satisfied the objection, for that matter, in works which are lost to us.) For example he writes, in another place than the one cited above, that tragic imitators imitate "men in action" (πράττοντας). Here he considers, as the object of the imitation which constitutes plot, neither action nor "character," but rather something like the "action of characters." This is more interesting: the idea seems to provide a bridge between plot and character. Or, more exactly speaking, the plans for a bridge. For Aristotle has given us no way to understand the kinetic principle of character, by which it may be transformed into action, by which "goodness" and the action of the "good" man may appear in their unity. But there is still another kind of observation in the *Poetics* which assures us of Aristotle's interest in a synthesis of plot with character. He prefers, as the character of the appropriate hero for a tragedy, a man who is good but who has some important flaw. It is precisely this flaw by which the hero falls when his fortune turns from good to bad. In other words, the man's character is an ingredient in what happens to him, in the action (or "passion") by which he falls. Could the imitation of the particular action ($\pi\rho\hat{a}\xi\iota\varsigma$)—that is, the imitation which makes that particular plot—not be also, at the same time, an imitation of the hero's character?

Aristotle failed to account suitably, in the *Poetics*, for the stubborn unity within the division of the parts of tragedy. What may surprise us especially, though, is not merely that Aristotle failed to *account* for the unity of the parts of tragedy, but that he did not discuss the peculiarly fruitful unity which exists between literary plot and literary character, a unity which is grounded in metaphysical relationships which deeply interested him, and which he treated with exemplary depth in other writings. This unity has, in fact, been seldom discussed by students of literature, precisely because it does involve metaphysics.

This kind of unity of plot, or action, and character in tragedy—or in literature in general, for this entire argument is broadly applicable—has direct and important analogies to the structure of existence. In fact, we can *best* understand that literary relationship by understanding the structure of existence which underlies it and serves as its model. Each of us is, as an individual, in one sense character (ἦθος). There is something in us by which we are of a certain sort (ποιός τις) rather than of some other sort. Perhaps we might call this something "personality." Here we will call it "character." This quality (ποιότης) which we are, or which is us, does not exist statically or timelessly. That through which one is of a certain sort need not be immobile, or outside of time. In fact it cannot be, for we exist, with all that we are, only within time. Our character exists only as enacted, used, introduced into time. It comes along with us, so to speak. Thus, of course, it also exists as relation to other aspects of what-is, of reality. Quality, despite Aristotle's suggestion in the *Poetics, can* enter into relationships. Let us take the example of our moral will, one of the clearest expressions of the character by which we are of a certain kind, by which we are quality. That will is always being confronted with new situations, thus being situated, temporally, in different configurations of what-is. We exist, as moral potential, both kinetically and "in relation" to other people, places, or, often, to that part of our own unity—our memory, our hope, our body—which may be relatively inactive in consciousness at a particular instant. So significant is this relational aspect of our moral existence that—to stress the point even harder—we appear to owe even our moral self-consciousness, our awareness of ourselves as responsible beings, to other people.

When we are infants other people point us out to ourselves: they name us, scold us, attempt to teach us—by calling our attention to what we have recently done, to that from which we can learn—and by multiple influences elicit from us an awareness of ourselves as potentials for "acting well" or "acting badly" (in their terms, of course). This active, and relational, situation of the moral expression of our character, as we live it, deserves close thought. And it, obviously, is only one aspect of character. We might make similar points about our aesthetic or rational ways of being: both of which ways are fundamentally relational, fusing character with the beautiful or the true. Yet even in terms of these preliminary remarks it would have to be strongly said that the relational situation of existence is only a context. Man's character ($\hat{\eta}\theta o s$) is not a static substance, a product of environment. We cannot admit the idea that society creates or fundamentally directs character. Rather character is an inalienable, unique way of handling and organizing the encountered world, a unique and consistent configuration of the happenings to which it is related, to which it relates itself. This active style is the style by which each person is, his personality: it marks, like linguistic style, all that "otherness" with which it transacts.

Action ($\pi \rho \hat{a} \xi \iota s$), as we know it in the structure of existence, is simply one form of the kinetic, relational situation of character. I am referring to the popular, and literary, sense of the word "action," not to the whole network of events which happen to and by character in the constituting of a life. "Action," here, is a form of character in which it creatively, that is transformingly, transacts with what-is. The relation of character to its actions—its transactions—is one of identity: character *is* its actions. To be sure, just as in the analysis of literature, character and action in existence are separable by analysis, but only artificially so. They are not separable in "reality." Character is really its actions, then, in somewhat the same sense in which form *is* its contents. We cannot claim that under actions ($\pi \rho \acute{a} \xi \epsilon \iota s$) lies a separable, independent agent, an $\hat{\eta}\theta o s$. Yet we may claim that, in those actions and one with them, an element of organization is present which in analysis can be thought of as a distinct emphasis within the whole. That element of organization is character ($\hat{\eta}\theta o s$).

The intimate relation of character to action, in existence, is the model for that relation as it appears in tragedy's—or any genre's—fusion of character and action. The word "model" needs explaining. The relation of literary creation to basic experience of existence is oblique and magical. The literary mind does not copy life, or a world "out-there." In fact, for the literary mind there is usually doubt about the very existence of a so-called "external world." We may say that a certain orientation within existence, a sense of the composition and intimate nature of existence, is what transfers itself, in the case before us, from "life" to literature. Literature is that deeply rooted in life. This transferal, which is of utmost importance to anyone concerned with what literature does to life, was certainly suspected by Aristotle, as I have suggested, for he wrote of plot as an imitation of men in action, that is, of men who were their action. Characters, embodied dynamically in action, are truly "men in action." And as such, familiar as they are to us, they form the subject of that "imitation" which constitutes, according to Aristotle, the plot of tragedy. Aristotle was not far from an adequate statement of his problem. We have seen, here, how the unified structure of existence, with its interplay of character and action, serves as model for the unity of ἦθος with μῦθος via πρᾶξις in tragedy, as Aristotle conceived tragedy. Aristotle needed—we may presume to say—a better appreciation of that unified structure, as it provides a model for literature.

The nature of this unity, as it expresses itself both in life and tragedy—for that matter in literature in general—may be suggested a final time by a grammatical analogy which Aristotle himself offers and which is of considerable verbal interest. The unity which concerns us revolves still about the notion of "men in action," that notion which seemed to draw the three elements of plot, action, and character into one. This notion, "men in action," is expressed in Greek by a participle, πράττοντας, in the plural and describes a characteristically participial situation, as distinct either from a substantive or a verbal situation. Man, as described here, has "character" or essence, but only to the extent that he puts it into act: like a participle, that is, his substance must be dynamized to exist. Man exists, then, as a verbalized substance, or a substantialized verb: in short, as a participle. Man is a participle. He is not completely substantialized—a noun, nor is he merely act—a verb. This particular conception of man in action describes a familiar situation of existence, and serves as a key to the unity of character with action with plot, whether in literature or in life.

8

SARTRE AND THE QUESTION OF CHARACTER IN LITERATURE

L'homme n'est rien que ce qu'il se fait....—SARTRE

i

I have argued that the relationship of lived life to its transformation into literature is ultimately inexplicable and magical; and accordingly, in the preceding chapter, I have dealt in analogy, not even to try to account for that relationship, but simply to make its potential explanation imaginable. A large equation has been constructed:

$$\frac{\text{character (in life)}}{\text{action (in life)}} \quad \cdot \quad \frac{\text{character (in literature)}}{\text{action (in literature)}}$$

In each realm character has been viewed as something realizing itself only in act, having no existence apart from the things it does. Yet it has seemed to merit a separate name, to be a unique and persistent style within the actions which compose an individual's life.

Thus the question of projection has so far, in this section, been handled indirectly, though I believe as directly as the topic permits. We are not going to be able to *show*, between the character of the author and the character in his work, the taking-place of the refined translation of life into art. That would be like trying to *see* the details of a complex chemical reaction; we see only the results.

I believe we can, though, come closer to a showing than in the previous essay, where the intention was introductory, to account for a dissatisfaction with Aristotelian theory. Closing in on the problem will be best done by considering the work of a man who has been both an analyst of character and a creator of literary characters. His "analysis of human character" will have to take the place of his own "character," about which we could hardly expect to be as well informed. The "analysis" will here indicate Sartre's view of the nature of human character, and it will do so with great sureness and clarity. By considering a few of his own works, subsequently, we can form some idea of how a notion of human character, and by implication a character itself (Sartre's), have passed over into literary characters.

L'Être et Le Néant is a hymn in praise of the insubstantial. In that book the substantial emerges as the great enemy. It is the inert, the viscous, the spiritless. It is the realm of death, both in our conventional, literal sense of that word, and in the broader sense of whatever is not active, vital, life at its most "authentic." Among substantial forms of existence, in this broader sense, Sartre includes such a notion as "selfhood." He does not deny that selfhood exists; on the contrary, he asserts its existence emphatically. It, and all other substantialities, alone has "being." But the "being" of selfhood is inert, lifeless. We see this in introspection, Sartre says. Our self exists only in the past. As "being" it can never be "becoming." Self is that essence which is lodged behind, even though in, us. That essence plays no part in the present of consciousness, the moving, insubstantial life which is what we distinctively are as living creatures.

Man's present, Sartre accordingly contends, is always completely undefined, unfettered by his past or substantial "self." The present is entirely free. It is not that there is no bridge at all between an individual's past and his present. Sartre's position is not that radical, for there is personal continuity. This continuity exists as what Sartre terms *"projet,"* or projection (casting forward) of goals for one's existence and of schemata of movements towards one's chosen goals. These goals pervade, and in the end serve to define, a person's existence. One is defined by his projection of himself towards the goal of being a great banker, a great cook, or a great philosopher. Yet these goals submit to revision at any moment. Man can change them. Such a change need not involve a radical revolution, though such a revolution is quite possible. Mere local change may occur: it serves to sever particular tributary fibers of the grand thread which connects one's present to his past, his becoming to his being. Yet it is also always possible, Sartre believes, completely to redirect one's "projet," to sever the grand thread. For example, the fact that a man has once espoused a particular religious or political position by no means prevents him from completely changing his position at any moment. Man is free. His becoming is arbitrarily linked to his being.

From this overall, radical freedom it follows, for Sartre, that man acquires a peculiar "moral" responsibility through the very structure of his existence. (Sartre denies that the notion of "morality" is relevant here, but we can hardly accept that denial.) Man is responsible, at every moment, for the way in which he exists, for the way and for what he becomes. No longer can he escape the burden of the present. It is he, after all, who guards and controls his own "self" retrospectively. Most important, it is he who maintains or changes his "projet." There is great weight on man's shoulders. It is not the weight of an external moral law which must be fulfilled. It is an inner weight: that of a choice waiting to be made. In order to live in consonance with this responsibility and the need to choose, which accompanies it, man must accept and assume his freedom. He must—Sartre tends easily to the imperative here—accept his selflessness, his protension. He must live all this. Action, in the broad sense of motion forward into the new, through experience, must be embraced.

It can be no surprise, to a reader of *L'Être et Le Néant*, to find that Sartre's fiction reflects an original view of character in literature. Character in the older-fashioned sense, where it means something as substantial as "selfhood," is interpreted precisely like selfhood and relegated to the past, Being. Room must consequently be made for a new view of character. Two of Sartre's best plays, *Les Mouches* and *Le Diable et le bon Dieu*, as well as his novel, *La Nausée*, will illustrate the importance, in Sartre's imaginative work, of his distinctly new philosophical view of the matter.

Les Mouches is thematically comparable to Aeschylus' *Oresteia* and to Sophocles' *Electra*. Sartre shows us Orestes coming, with his teacher, to Argos, at the beginning of the play. The city is infested with flies. It is the day before the national festival of the dead, which was instituted after the murder of Agamemnon, in order to help the citizens repent. On that day, the dead emerge from a large cave to descend on the city, visit with their descendants, and fortify the people's sense of guilt for the killing of Agamemnon. Clytemnestra and Aegisthus promote this state of affairs by pious references to their own guilt and to the need for expiation. They also fasten an iron rule onto the citizens. Orestes comes into this situation.

The play itself concerns Orestes' discovery, in this context, of a way to realize his freedom. He is a well-mannered young man who has thought much and asked little: the result is that, although like all men he is bound to freedom, he has not accepted, begun to control, that situation. After he has discussed the situation in Argos with Electra, he realizes that it has a unique relevance to his development. The curse which his mother has brought down on his family and on the whole city appears to him, gradually, to be an unavoidable obstacle in his own way. He cannot sidestep it. It is this realization, coming after conversation with Electra, and exposure to the glorious annual ceremony of repentance, which fosters Orestes' decision to remove the obstacle, to kill his mother and her lover. This he does, making clear to them that he is acting not only in the name of his freedom, but in opposition to their self-indulgent lifetime of repentance. After the killing, Orestes and Electra both flee to the sanctuary of Apollo, where the Erinyes find them. Waking in the morning, brother and sister are beset by the nauseating agents of primitive vendetta. By now—quite in contrast to the beginning of the play—it is Electra, not Orestes, who feels on the outside of, disengaged from, the central issues of the action. The killing, with its responsibilities and consequences, has been Orestes', and to him is reserved the courage to contest the Erinyes and even Zeus, who appears to offer salvation to the two mortals. Zeus's condition is that Orestes should devote his own life to repentance, even if only nominal, so that the Argives will continue to fear the gods and be a people of slavering cowards. But Orestes, insisting that he is now beyond even the god's control, refuses. In the ultimate assertion of his freedom he strides out through the citizens of the city, the Erinyes clinging to him like bats, and disappears, symbolically taking with him, as it were, the pollution of the city.

Sartre's conclusion is lyrical and potent. It offers us, in certain respects, a picture of the Sartrean man well integrated into art: Orestes grows into a sense of his freedom through discovering a means to achieving it; he then assumes responsibility for his acts, even in the face of Zeus, and thus embraces the whole situation of his freedom; and finally, in his actions, he accepts the dangerous insubstantiality of freedom wholeheartedly. Yet we are left, after all, in confusion.

The problem, I believe, is this: we are not certain whether Orestes is striving to realize his freedom or to free Argos of pollution and his family from corruption. To be sure, as far as through the actual killing of Clytemnestra and Aegisthus, Orestes appears to be striving for both these goals: there is a perfect equation between his self-assertion and his dealing with a critical situation. The demand made on Orestes by the degrading, savior-needing condition of *his* city and *his* people is an explicit directing of Orestes in his path towards self-realization. Argos calls him. Our problem begins after the killing, the point at which, it will be remembered, Aeschylus turned his *Oresteia* over to the gods, the *Eumenides* being essentially worked out on the supernatural plane. Sartre's Orestes is left, at that point, with only two things to do: to revel in his freedom and to defy menacers of that freedom. With the boast, *"Je suis ma liberté,"* Orestes throws himself into the enjoyment of his self-conquest, exulting in his freedom. At the same time, he refuses the differing efforts of Zeus and Electra to make him remain in Argos, to rule and consolidate his victory. Zeus wants a new authority to keep his people abject, while Electra, who has by now been intimidated by murder and the Erinyes, only wants Orestes to remain near her, to protect her. She is awe-struck by the new power freed in her brother: again, she hardly recognizes him. But Orestes will no longer be fettered. He departs, taking the Erinyes with him, moving again freely, into the blue. Even though he is setting an example of freedom for his people in this way, we feel—as far as Orestes is concerned —that he is simply indulging himself in a deep solution of freedom. The plot, the problem or situation originally facing Orestes, has run out, and we have only Orestes with a contentless freedom before him.

Clearly we are faced here with one consequence of Sartre's

new notion of "character." Orestes exists as act. He makes a choice—of his goal or direction—and proceeds to enact his choice. He does this without having any character in the older-fashioned sense, without being burdened or chained, in the present, by the fetters of character. He is all *projet*. The only anchor, within the play, for Orestes' action is the situation of Argos, which he initially confronts. When his confrontation with this situation ends, he is without anchor. It is then, I believe, that Sartre's hero is weakened by lack of substantial character. Had he been portrayed with such character, Orestes would not have seemed, in his mere, windy freedom, to be an unattached spirit, essentially out of touch with the plot of *Les Mouches* and so a partially disunifying element.

ii

In *Le Diable et le bon Dieu,* Sartre offers us an extensive study-through-behavior of Gœtz with less elaborate analysis of many other individuals. The play is rich in dramatized points of view, each of them supported by lively conversation. The dialectical interplay between the archbishop and the banker, between Heinrich and Nasty, or between Gœtz and any of his adversaries—Catharine, Heinrich, Nasty—is masterfully vital.

It will be remembered that Gœtz, a professional general in the hire of the archbishop, is besieging Worms. Gœtz is known for his cruelty and military skill: we see him feared on both sides. The archbishop cannot trust his own general, and dreads a brutal ransacking of Worms; such destruction would harm the rich burgers of the city, and thus weaken the support of the archbishop. Heinrich and Nasty, in Worms, are equally uncertain of what Gœtz will do and are afraid for the clergy and the common people, respectively. One feels, before encountering Gœtz, that in him must reside a nature of iron, an unshakable quality. Yet from our first encounter we sense, in Gœtz, a mercurial behavior, something other than a self of any precise sort, and an unfirm commitment to killing. It is as though he were acting a part, projecting an ideal for his existence. This suspicion is confirmed in the critical conversation among Gœtz, Heinrich, and Nasty at the end of Act I. Gœtz is about to leave for the night assault on Worms, in which 20,000 citizens' lives will presumably be lost. Over-dramatizing his undertaking, no doubt through uncertainty of his real nature, Gœtz claims that he is a man who makes even God ill at ease: *"Je suis l'homme qui met le Tout-Puissant mal à l'aise."* It is precisely here that Heinrich, sensing the hollowness of Gœtz's boast, reminds him of the evil of all men and of the absurdity in believing oneself supremely or uniquely diabolical. If one wants to excel, Heinrich insists, one had better choose goodness rather than evil. To Gœtz this argument seems partly convincing, partly intriguing: he is overwrought. The possibility of changing his existence strikes him as refreshing. In a burst of enthusiasm for a new way to excel, he rolls dice to see whether he should decide for evil or goodness. At the will of the dice (loaded, according to Catharine) he decides for the good. He has reversed his *projet.*

It is unnecessary, here, to discuss the rest of this play—the way Gœtz embraces a "saintly" life, attempts to help the common people of Worms and its region, and ultimately, still dreaded for his former ferocity, forsakes even his "saintly" existence to revert to a military life, a mere life, this time without belief or interest in God. For Sartre's point is clear at the end of the first act, when a throw of the dice has "determined" Gœtz's projection. Or rather we see Sartre there expressing, again in literary form, a conviction which appears in his philosophy: the conviction that a valid life is something to be given existence only through action and ever-renewed decision. Gœtz is, we might say, at the mercy of his decisions, as Orestes was at the mercy of his. Admittedly the situation in *Le Diable et le bon Dieu* is different. For in that play there is essentially no plot, or situation, apart from Gœtz; so we never feel with him, as we do with Orestes, that his action falls out of relation to a plot. In that respect, it may seem, *Le Diable* is a more successful play than *Les Mouches*. Yet we must be troubled, with Gœtz, over the whole problem of the disincarnated, utterly protending literary figure. We cannot claim that Sartre is a dupe of his own literary creation here, for he prepares us to accept the waywardness and unfettered freedom of Gœtz, as he had of Orestes. Gœtz himself is sufficiently aware of the unexpectedness of his change, so that we follow him into it. We *can* complain, though, that the abrupt re-projections of Gœtz deprive him, as a literary figure, of some significance and intelligibility. After all there is, as Plato believed, a connection between *stasis* and knowledge.

iii

It may seem inappropriate, in this context, to consider *La Nausée*. Only at his publisher's request did Sartre decide to call that work a *roman* rather than a *journal intime*. Thus, in a sense, Sartre may seem to exempt himself in that work from the obligation even to consider plot and character in a usual fictional way. It is nonetheless true, however, that the success of that work depends on the relation of Roquentin to the world around him, thus to a series of experiences, if not precisely to a plot. That relationship concerns us here.

Roquentin is comparable to Orestes or Gœtz only because he, too, has no fixed "character." In *La Nausée* there is ample opportunity to reveal this lack of character, however, whereas in *Les Mouches* and *Le Diable* we were simply and briskly shown the dramatis personae in action and then left to draw our own conclusions about them. There is some affinity, furthermore, between Roquentin and Camus' Meursault, in *L'Étranger*. Not only does neither of those figures have "character," in the conventional literary sense, but each of them exists, in a pre-eminent degree, simply as the experiences which he "has" or passively submits to. That in itself is a remarkable similarity. Yet to draw a distinction here may also be useful. Meursault remains—at least until the conclusion of *L'Étranger*—devoid of self-consciousness. The events in which he plays a part simply make "impressions" on him, but he cannot reflect on them, or draw them into the center of his consciousness. Roquentin, on the other hand, is far more self-conscious, and in the context of *La Nausée* emerges as a metaphysician, simply by virtue of taking his own experiences seriously. *La Nausée* becomes, as a consequence, a biography of lived philosophy, though not a biography of a person or "character" living that philosophy.

In illustration of this point we may remind ourselves of three central scenes in *La Nausée*. A point at which we find Roquentin's salient trait, his lack of *caractère*, most thoroughly dramatized, occurs in his visit to the museum and art gallery of Bouville. There he sees the pictures of the men and women who "made Bouville great" in the previous century. They were—or are portrayed as—solid, middle-class citizens, prosperous, decorously concerned with culture and self-satisfied. At the end of his visit, Roquentin calls these painted men *salauds*. And throughout we know that he despises them. Yet the reason for his hatred is typically subtle. It is metaphysical, not precisely political, or social. We see only later to what extent Roquentin considers human existence, as a whole, non-existence, something *de trop*, extending "out from" reality. In the passage before us we see Roquentin facing the imposture of men who tried to turn their non-existence into a most stable form of existence. Those men took the standards of their society—its bourgeois notions of virtue, honor, and success—as so many guarantees of the absolute value of their accomplishments and behavior. They were guilty of systematic and totally self-centered *mauvaise foi*, for which Roquentin hates them.

Of peculiar interest to us is the way Sartre employs this
scene to convey Roquentin's sense of his own nothingness,
his lack of "substance." We are aware continually that his
hatred for the makers of Bouville extends, at least in the form
of scorn, to himself. Roquentin is no self-satisfied hater. Indeed, in the presence of so much bourgeois "weight," he feels
his own flimsiness with particular intensity. Self-consciousness, for him, is frequently just such a consciousness of "nothingness."

A comparable awareness of his own lack of character, and
thus a dramatization of that lack, with accompanying sense
of the presence of the contents of his experience, is evident,
near the end of *La Nausée*, when Roquentin goes to the
Jardin Public at night. We need only insist on the general
features of that much-discussed experience. More deeply than
in the art gallery, Roquentin realizes here in the garden the
falsity of the attempts of civilization to impose its own
standards and descriptions on reality. A critique of language
is basic here. It becomes evident to Roquentin that the names
of the natural things in the garden *are* not those things.
*"Noire? J'ai senti le mot qui se dégonflait, qui se vidait de son
sens avec une rapidité extraordinaire. Noire? La racine
n'était pas noire, ce n'était pas du noir qu'il y avait sur ce
morceau de bois—c'était ... autre chose...."* The whole
natural reality of the garden comes on Roquentin as a powerful sub-linguistic presence. For reasons which we must largely
supply with our feelings, this awareness in Roquentin establishes a sense of the arbitrary reality about him. Trees, flow-
ers, and leaves, in losing that appearance of substantiality
which we confer on them through our language, and through
all the expectations which accompany our use of words, assume their true nature. We know them, Roquentin says, as
de trop, unnecessary, dispensable. In this knowing, Roquentin once more understands *his own* unnecessariness. *"Et
moi—veule, alangui, obscène, digérant, ballotant de mornes*

pensées—moi aussi j'étais de trop." Being, and knowing that
one is *de trop*, in this sense, clearly fits Sartre's idea of being
in the "human condition." To that extent, Roquentin may
appear here as a kind of Sartrean Everyman.

Equally Sartrean is Roquentin's weakly expressed desire
to find some salvation from his insubstantial state. Roquentin
has, throughout the course of his diary entries, been writing a
diary of Rollebon. Shortly after the awareness in the Jardin
Public he starts to doubt the possibility of such a biography.
How can one person make himself responsible, Roquentin
wonders, for another's existence: each existence is arbitrary,
without cause, *simply there*. It occurs to him that art is perhaps the firmest compensation for one's uncertain condition.
Roquentin is drawn by the possibility, suggested by Sartre
himself in *Qu'est-ce que la littérature,* that one creates in
order to represent the world as it is, but as though freedom
were its source. The work of art thus created becomes a formal, but functional, cosmos of its own. Roquentin's own
impulse toward such creation comes, externally at least, from
hearing a Negress singing, on a jazz record,

> Some of these days
> You'll miss me honey.

He thinks of the people—the Jewish composer, the Negress—
who have made themselves responsible for new existence
through that record, and who have thus done something to
justify their own existence. This thought is so potent to
Roquentin that he wonders, at the close of *La Nausée,*
whether he could now write a novel. On this note—one of the
few positive notes of the work—Sartre leaves us, not with a
feeling that Roquentin may now escape from "characterlessness," but with a sense that he may now strive, through his
characterlessness, for some end. Yet in that striving, the argument seems to be, the *de-trop*-ness of Roquentin would be
alleviated only in the past. He would be able to think back,

with some pride, to his past. But his present, and of course his future, would continue to be nothingness and the frontier of nothingness, respectively.

iv

These analyses could have been directed at almost any of Sartre's creative works: his philosophy of character is pervasive. We would have found, in such plays as *Huis-clos, Morts sans sépultures,* or *La Putain respectueuse,* the suppression of substantial character and the emphasis on action which we have noticed in *Les Mouches* and *Le Diable et le bon Dieu.* Each of those plays is pre-eminently a drama of "situaation," turning on the abrupt projection of character into an unexpected, more or less unintelligible, context which demands original action.

In *Huis-clos,* the three damned ones are thrown into an unendurable proximity to one another, in a world without décor. Nothing substantial remains; they are in the hell of unrestricted human emotions. The general situation in *Morts sans sépultures* is comparable; there all is suspense, protending towards an indefinite, apparently certain catastrophe. In both of these plays, admittedly, the cast have more *distinctive* personalities than have Orestes, Gœtz, or Roquentin. But those personalities are not permitted to rest, to *be*—in the pejorative Sartrean sense; rather they are ruthlessly thrown forward into situations where they must improvise. So with the characters in *La Putain respectueuse.* Lizzie, Fred, and the Negro may seem more like character-types than we are accustomed to find in Sartre. Yet whatever is stock, and thereby pre-defined, in them is left behind in the restless haste of the action.

In Sartre's prose fiction there is no better embodiment of his view of character than Mathieu, in *Les Chemins de la liberté.* Marcelle sizes up her lover at the outset of *L'Âge de raison:*

Eh bien, dit-elle, c'est toujours ta fameuse lucidité, tu es amusant, mon vieux, tu as une telle frousse d'être ta propre dupe que tu refuserais la plus belle aventure du monde plutôt que de risquer de te mentir.

Bien oui, dit Mathieu, tu le sais bien. Il y a longtemps qu'on l'a dit.

It is an old story; one which will be developed throughout Sartre's series of novels: Mathieu meets a German attack fully conscious, in the midst of furious shooting, that he is firing on all the tentativeness which has restricted him throughout his life. The result of Mathieu's continual self-analysis is that he is translucent, without solidity, mere consciousness. In short, he is content—and more than that—with the kind of characterlessness, insubstantiality, from which Daniel, in that same series, feels initial aversion. As a homosexual, Daniel is keenly aware of his "category," of the status to which society is anxious to consign him. It is with a certain horrified pride, then, that he announces his secret to Mathieu at the end of *L'Âge de raison.* But in that very scene he is frustrated: Mathieu is insufficiently shocked, not eager enough to adopt the new method of defining Daniel. He helps Daniel to realize that he, Daniel, *is* not a homosexual. He *is,* as Sartre would say, not anything.

Sartre's short stories reflect this same notion of character. The collection *Le Mur* (1939) offers us a gallery of insubstantial, highly self-aware beings, whose distinctive natures are difficult either to discover or to remember. The title story provides an illustration. Ibbetia has, as far as the story presents him, no past. He and the other two *condamnés* are three configurations of will and response which find themselves in a situation which they have no special qualifications to understand. The single fact of death is all that matters to any of them. Nor have the main figures of *Erostrate* or *Intimité* any weight. However, the final story in the collection, *L'Enfance d'un chef,* involves an effective variation on this

Sartrean theme. Lucien, like Daniel in *Les Chemins de la liberté*, is anxious to grow identical with himself, to *be*. He is not simply anxious, like Daniel, to be one of the categories by which society defines men; rather he becomes increasingly determined, through the course of his *enfance*, to be an entire social role, that of the capitalistic leader. We follow this growing intention of Lucien, through his disgust with Bergère, his new respect for his father and family, his possession of a mistress—a "conventional" capitalistic act—and finally —the true mark of self-discovery, in his case—the affiliation with Action Française. This path toward the adoption of a role is difficult for Lucien, as indeed the description of it seems to be for Sartre, whose handling of the *development* of the theme is awkward. What interests us especially, though, is the severity of Sartre's judgment here. Clearly his Lucien is a caricature of a man of *mauvaise foi*, of one who is trying to hide his insubstantial nature for himself. We follow the growth of a fundamental self-deception, the dramatization of which is simply one more proof, in Sartre's terms, of the insubstantiality of life.

v

What, finally, are we entitled to conclude about the value and significance of Sartre's conception of literary character? We have touched, already, on certain aesthetic difficulties in *Les Mouches* and *Le Diable et le bon Dieu*. It appeared that a certain intelligibility—in a general sense—was lost by the total volatilization of character into its acts, experiences, or reflections. In the case of *Les Mouches* we raised the question of the relation of plot to insubstantial character: there seemed to be a dangerous independence of such character from any underlying theme. In a longer critique, these questions could have been addressed to *La Nausée*. A certain vagueness spreads out from Roquentin over the entire organization of his book. Structurally this is clear. The book has no beginning or end. It lacks the "plot" on which, in one sense, meaningful literary experiences depend. Inevitably, the book *seems* arbitrarily put together. Here, again, we feel that Sartre's experimentation has involved an artistic loss. To a greater or less degree a comparable loss is apparent in those other works of Sartre to which we have alluded.

Yet the main intention, here, has not been to evaluate Sartre's success in dealing originally with the question of literary character. In a sense, the value—or lack of it—of that achievement is less important than another issue: that in all of the works mentioned here—and particularly in the three to which most attention was devoted—Sartre is experimenting with a literary method which is itself of intrinsic interest. The radical quality of this experiment needs to be emphasized. We may well hesitate to call Sartre's suppression and rehandling of character in literature simply an original literary technique. It does, to be sure, mark a stage in a technical revolt against the full-blooded nineteenth-century fictional character, as we find him in Balzac, Dickens, or Thackeray. But we are dealing, in Sartre, with an entire reorganization of the novelist's sensibility. That is more important. In Sartre's own case this reorganization has a distinctive origin. Philosophical conviction and literary practice converge: they rise from the single source of a distinctive apprehension of the nature of reality. That basic apprehension, or sensibility, is an awareness of the insubstantiality of lived life and of the substantial inertia of character. Though we must, of course, judge Sartre's fiction from the text, not on the basis of its foundations in a kind of consciousness, still we will find it worth while to meditate on the degree of worth of Sartre's basic experience of life and character. For we will, in that way, not only have a key to the understanding of much of Sartre's own fiction, but we will be exercising our understanding of the kind of metaphysical awareness out of which conventional as well as Sartrean fiction is made.

Part IV

9

LITERATURE INSIDE OUT

There all the barrel-hoops are knit,
There all the serpent-tails are bit,
There all the gyres converge in one,
There all the planets drop in the Sun.—YEATS

The present argument runs itself, by the honest course of its development, into a very substantial complication. I should like here to unravel a knot and to rope a few more problems with the remaining ends.

I have been dealing with two different rhythms of activity which affect the making of works of literature. The first chapters concerned themselves with introjection, the process of drawing-up the world, or at least the world-just-turned-into-human-understanding, so that it could enter the work of literature. The dominant image there was of an in-drawing by which the creator induced the world into his creation. Something like this event would seem, to an inexperienced but perceptive critic, to be the primal literary activity for which an account is required. The world of words obviously takes its starting-point in the world that words are about. Yet that "about" is crucial. In the following discussions I consider a more immediate source, for literature, than the world that literature's words are "about." I concern myself with deep psychological factors and with the question of character; both of which seem to be parts of an "inner world," quite different from the "outer world" which was the first source of names; and both of which were eager to lay a claim—that the "inner" was the chief factor in the making of literature. Beyond this rivalry of claims lay the always important question about literature: whether its affiliations are more with the outer world, the world of "objective realities," or whether they are with the inner world of imagination.

Suppose we say that first introjection, then projection, are required, and in that order, to create the literary work. In one sense there will be no quarrel. If the "outer world" is interpreted broadly, to include not only nameable things, but encounterable ideas and impressions beyond the individual self, then clearly that world is the first source of material for literature. It provides materials. We can then say that the human psyche domesticates those materials, readying and refining them in language; and that subsequently, after much inner labor, it produces what was once a world as a highly transmuted creation of its own, doing so from the matrix of its own internal laws, its psychic necessities. The world and the self thus follow each other in a simple, if laborious, process of contribution to literature.

This description is unrealistic. As argued in the first chapter, error is near whenever we discuss our world, the world *we* are in, as though it had an existence outside our language. What is the "tree" for us, after all, before we fashion some sound to designate it, to "indicate" it with spirit? What is the sound of that tree falling, even, before we emit some sound which "stands for" it, or at least expresses it? The tree and the sound of its fall are not non-existent before naming. The tree is deep in an existence which is nature's, and which we language makers can never hope to know on its own terms. The sound of the falling tree was there before there were human ears to hear it, but it existed, I guess, without overtones or affective qualities. It was non-existent by human standards. The world, in any sense in which it is a meaning-

ful factor in literature, is colored and worked over by psyche
from the beginning.

The notion of psyche, too, must here be given its full range,
so that we see how inextricably involved world and self are,
from the outset of their transaction. The drawing up of a
tree into the word "tree" is not simply an act of intellect. It
involves a whole person. We could here return to the argument of Adrian Stokes, considered earlier. There it appeared
that the human struggle to adopt a "healthy" relation to the
outer world begins in infancy, with the relation to the breast.
The libidinal factors at work in that adjustment would un-
doubtedly influence the child's approach to language, in
those early years of naming. Descent into details, here, would
only reveal my difficulties with the question; but I presume
that the quality of a word, for the child, from the outset assumes a relation to the way he pronounces it; to where it falls
on his palate and to the position of his lips in saying it. It
seems evident that such relationships to language, thus to
the world named in language, are deeply tinged by kinds of
pleasure (or displeasure) provided by certain infant relationships to the breast. So thoroughly is the original apprehension
of the world, through language, not what we call "intellec-
tual." So profoundly is it domesticated into the economy of
purely human emotions.

The other side of all this is the "worldliness" which persists in the developed human uses of language, specifically
in the projection of that language into literary form. Both
tropes and certain dispositions—such as the sado-masochistic,
or that involved in adult problems with "projection"—seemed
earlier to be expressions of the distinctively human situation.
A psychoanalysis of history has been attempted, but never of
nature; nature has no neuroses. Yet nature, as raw material
in language, persists strongly; we only fail to sense its presence.

Here, a little said must stand for much. A great deal depends on the capacity for feeling the "thingliness" of language, for feeling the tree behind "tree." Everything militates against such feeling, in the course of a society's development with language; just as progress within a society is progress away from nature. The chief adversary of this "feeling" is the easy habit of falling into "the situation of language"—an example of what Sartre, in *Qu'est-ce que la littérature,* calls being *dans une situation.* In that situation we live language perfectly unconsciously, uttering it almost as though it were an extension of our own bodies. It is never experienced at a remove from us, palpable and out there. The gift of this awareness, according to Sartre, marks the true poet; for him alone language is tangible. In this sense poetry still retains a salvational force. It can lead us back to awareness of the character and composition of language.

The deepest trope, or most civilized neurosis, will find itself into literature via language which is half world. The stubborn feel of things will cling to its nouns. Images summoned by complex paragraphs, using all the "parts of speech," will smell and taste of the world. This will be known only subliminally, or in an act of direct reflection; it can hardly be a conscious element in the ordinary living of language. How real this knowledge is, however, can be illustrated by a simple experiment. We might castrate our speech of all words which referred to a world beyond us, to "things" or "thoughts" for whose existence man is in no way responsible. All the outer material of language might be purged. We would be left with a mouthful of sounds; sounds with no stubbornness, or resistance, in them. The world exists, in language, as resistance.

We find that the "world," stubbornly present in language and literature, exists there at every stage. Through the "thingliness" of the words it becomes, it invades the most intimate expressions of selfhood, neurosis, or basic trope. At the same time selfhood, the radically human, is present in every en-

counter with the "other" which it will plunder as the chief
source of linguistic material. The "world beyond the human"
is non-existent for the human. The literary work will have,
therefore, a dual composition reminiscent of that described
by Heidegger. In the completed piece of literature, "work"
and "earth" will resemble the elements contributed, in this
discussion, by "self" and "world." And between the two
pairs of elements there will be a similar tension, strengthening and deepening the artifact.

The dual rhythms of introjection and projection can also,
now, be accounted for more adequately. We can avoid the
disquietingly facile picture of an indrawing of the world,
through language, and a subsequent projection of that world,
internalized to the self's exigencies, into the literary creation.
All this, I believe, occurs in the career of Being from the
outer world into the work of literature. But it occurs with a
double complexity. Self and the world-for-man are inextricably interinvolved at every stage of this career. Furthermore
the double rhythm in which they deepen their marriage is
only misleadingly represented by our chronological description. The self has begun to project into verbal constructions,
literature in embryo, long before it has finished its raid on the
world, for words. (If that raid ever ends; and it need never.)
It is continually returning to the thingliness of things, to
find new blood for words and to draw in that blood. Thus the
two rhythms are endlessly interlocked.

10

ARISTOTLE AND THE SOURCE OF THE ARTWORK

> *The Rules of Aristotle are nothing but Nature and Good Sense reduced to a Method.*—JOHN DENNIS

As we have seen, the exact source of the work of art, the place from which it is born, is a matter for serious discussion. Is the outer world, the so-called "real," public world outside us the source? Or is some fusion, or combination, of the outer world and the artist's mind what we must look for? Artists, who have had the experience necessary to form a judgment on this matter, provide little assistance. The problem is buried so deep inside them that they cannot see it clearly. While philosophers, who may have the terminology and acumen needed for this problem, generally lack the experience. For these reasons, the source of the artwork has been neglected in aesthetic thought. This neglect is regrettable; it deflects attention from the similar but broader problem of the relation of art to the world which art "represents." Whether that "represented" world be viewed as "outer" or "inner," or even as transcendent, it must become art, must be *engendered,* at some point in the artist's transaction with reality. The crucial and delicate point at which the world becomes art, in this sense, is the source of the artwork. If we ignore the question

118

of the source of the artwork, we necessarily fail to grasp the general problem of how art is related to the world. While, on the contrary, once we have dealt seriously with the question of the source of artworks, we will have a tough double advantage: of immunity to facile statements about the relation of art to nature; and of authentic insight into that relation.

It is especially useful to study Aristotle's view of the source of artworks. I wish aesthetic systems were more often passed through the fire of this test; in no other way can their hard-headedness and firmness be better assessed. There is another incentive for studying Aristotle in these terms. In considering the source of art he adopts a complex and, historically speaking, significant transitional position. The complexity results from his uncertainty about the kind or degree of "externality" of the art work, whether it is literary or visual art. (As well as from his lack of direct concern with this problem as a problem.) On the one hand he seems to suggest—always with qualifications and never quite unambiguously—that the artist's mind is the sole source of art. We can sample this suggestion. On the other hand, through the overall tenor of the *Poetics,* he reminds us continually of the external reference of the work of art. He keeps our minds on the things in art which resemble things in the world. We feel the tension of his argument. By considering this tension we may come to appreciate more accurately Aristotle's view of the entire relation of art to nature. That view has often been obscured by the false clarity of his interpreters. Aristotle has too often been made more accessible and systematic than he is. Many of his interpreters have turned, in their arguments, to his statement that poetry is more "philosophical" than history because poetry deals with the universal rather than with the particular. That difficult observation has been taken simply as an edifying assertion of the nobility of art, and of the way in which art is an "improvement" on nature, or on the "real" world in general. As good a critic as Butcher comments that the truth, then, of poetry is essentially different from the truth of fact. . . .

or that it is

more profoundly true than those daily occurences which we can with confidence predict.

But such statements, of dubious value even as interpretations of the poetic universal, are seriously misleading when it comes to Aristotle's overall view of the relation of art to nature. They overlook that view Aristotle expressed in the *Physics*, when he said that the productions of nature are more perfect than those of art.

Aristotle's was a mind of great complexity, prone, like Plato's, to continual self-qualification. Aristotle's different works stand to each other in that dialectical relationship in which Plato's arguments, within a single work, stand to each other.

i

In chapter 25 of the *Poetics* Aristotle wrote:

It is less serious for a painter not to know that a female deer has no horns than to represent one inartistically.

This statement appears in the midst of a general discussion of artistic imitation. Aristotle here tries, as precisely as any-where in the *Poetics,* to explain the sense in which he con-siders imitation the basis of art. In this passage he makes an important distinction between two kinds of error which may occur in the art of poetry. One of these errors, he says, rises from an essential failing in the artist as artist: this is a failure to imitate successfully what one chooses to imitate. This failure goes to the heart of the artist's enterprise, en-tirely depriving it of value. The second error is less serious: it occurs if

he [the artist] makes a mistake about what he chooses to imitate or writes of impossible things—for example, a horse that moves both its right legs forward at the same time, or the faults that can occur in dealing with every one of the arts, as a mistake about medicine, or something in any other art whatever. . . .

Such an error does not argue serious weakness in the artist's use of his art. It shows a rather incidental weakness, aesthetically speaking. Aristotle seems here to consider it more important to imitate artistically than to imitate "scientifically," with detailed fidelity to the "outer world." If the choice must be made, it is more important to represent a female deer artistically than accurately.

Aristotle does not elaborate this argument at this point, and we are left with some doubt about his full meaning. After all he was attacking Plato here, and for that very reason limited his main point to a familiar Platonic issue: that of the relation between the poet and the things or "themes" in the world about which the poet writes. We were concerned earlier with the *Ion*. It will be remembered that Socrates there raised the question whether the poet has adequate knowledge of the things about which he writes. Did Homer know about military strategy, or horsemanship, or navigation when he wrote of them? Or would he need to admit, in each case, that the appropriate specialist—general, horseman, or sailor—had more adequate knowledge than the poet? Plato's conclusion is that the "specialist" would have truer knowledge and that the poet has only second-hand knowledge. In the *Republic* this problem is taken up again, under the general heading of "imitation." There Plato asserts that the poet is far removed from the Ideas, those principles of intelligibility which govern the Platonic universe. The poet is a copier of things—of the whole "external" world as far as man is concerned—which are themselves only copies or reflections of the Ideas. In this case, again, the poet is farther removed from the truth of things than are specialists—cobblers or saddle-makers—who are producers of real shoes and saddles which imitate the Ideas of shoes and saddles, respectively. It appears again that the poet, in his own craft, does not deal in knowledge. To this position, as it is variously defended by Plato, Aristotle simply replies here that exact reproduction of the "outer world" is not the chief criterion of poetic success, but that the adequate imitation of "what the poet chooses to imitate" is more important. Accuracy plus artistry would be best, Aristotle seems to imply, but artistry alone is preferable to accuracy alone.

Yet he implies more than is evident in this guarded countering of Plato. Although Aristotle *is* saying what is necessary for the argument, that to be inaccurate is less serious for the artist than to be inartistic, he implies more. In describing the less serious of these two errors, Aristotle discusses the case in which "he [the artist] makes a mistake about what he chooses to imitate or writes of impossible things. . . ." What is "what he chooses to imitate?" It may be some perceivable, or at least "externally" experienceable, entity which might have been imitated accurately but which the artist perceives (and imitates) inaccurately. Is this entity—let us say the "real" table—still the same entity when the artist has thus mistakenly perceived it? Is the table which the artist sees with five legs, instead of with four, still the table? Or is it not rather the table-as-experienced-by-the-artist? Is not the very object of imitation itself transmuted, aesthetically, if not—and here the question grows difficult—ontologically? There is a further interpretation which is imaginable, in the case of "what he [the artist] chooses to imitate." This interpretation seems to fit Aristotle's example of the female deer. We do not suppose that the artist who chooses to imitate that deer, and who is to err concerning her horns, actually looks at the deer in order to imagine it. The artist, in this case, is more likely to construct a deer imaginatively, and synthetically, on the basis of his experience of deers—and perhaps of other beings and shapes, too. The deer which he chooses to imitate, in this case, will not be a real-deer-as-experienced-by-the-artist;

rather it will be what we might imprecisely call an "ideal deer," a resolution of many experienced "real" deers. Thus, in either of the two senses which we can give to the phrase "what he [the artist] chooses to imitate," we find Aristotle implying not only that "scientific" accuracy is inessential to art, but also that artistic imitation need not choose as its object any entity in the "real" world, the "external" world out there. (Although the existence of that external world is never called in question.) It is implied, at least, not only that the artist may not "interpret" reality, but that he may not even take reality, in a broad, "external" sense, as his starting point.

This implication is further stressed by the suggestion that the artist may "write of impossible things," such as a "horse that moves both its right legs forward at the same time. . . ." Such an inaccurate description, presumably, may still be artistic. Yet it is patently based on a state of affairs which cannot exist, out-there, in the "real" world. The painted horse which moves its right legs simultaneously is no more nor less an "interpretation" of anything "real," than is the painted female deer with horns. In one sense—although a limited one —this impossible horse is spawned by the mind.

Even in these brief passages in chapter 25 of the *Poetics,* we see the sketching out—no more—of certain new possibilities for aesthetic thought. At the time of their forging, those possibilities promised far more than a revision of the Platonic primacy of the "thing" over the artist who imitates it. It is inadequate to claim that imitation, for Aristotle, is "not an imitation of an idea in the mind of the artist." For Aristotle appears to be moving toward that kind of imitation although he never arrives, and perhaps never wished to arrive, at the notion of real aesthetic autonomy, of what we have come to call "the aesthetic realm."

ii

In a relevant and more familiar sequence of thoughts, Aristotle refers several times to his belief that tragedy is an "imitation of better men than our contemporaries." He does not mean, by this, that tragedy imitates our ancestors, men who have lived before. Who, then, are these "better men"? Aristotle gives two chief answers to this question. In chapter 15, he writes that

the dramatists should imitate good portrait painters who, though presenting the right form and making their portraits like the originals, make them more beautiful.

It is clear that he is here thinking of art simply as an "interpretation" of its object, an interpretation in which the object is primary, the main matter. The "betterness" of the men so represented, we might say, is added by the artist; it would not reside in the men themselves. Yet the artist's addition would be made solely in terms of the men: it would have to be continuous with *their* appearance.

Elsewhere Aristotle expresses differently this matter of "whom the tragedy imitates." Recurring to the example of the painter Zeuxis, who painted men "better than they are," he writes in chapter 25:

Perhaps it is impossible that men should be such as Zeuxis painted them, but it is better for them to be superior to the reality, because the artist ought to improve on his model.

This notion that the "artist ought to improve on his model" is familiar from the preceding citation. But there is a new note this time. It seems possible that men, as they "really" are, may never to any degree provide the material for Zeuxis' idealistic paintings. When Aristotle says that "it is better for them [men] to be superior to the reality," he evidently means by men, "men who have been turned into art by Zeuxis." What are the models of these art-men? Are the models "real men" to whom the artist has added? We seem to be faced with a *different kind of men* entirely—not just in the sense that Zeuxis' men are in art, not in life—but in the additional sense that Zeuxis' men have different "souls," are "ontologically" of a higher order.

This implication, concerning the way men find their ways into the plots of tragedy, may profitably be studied in a similar and related context; in terms of Aristotle's concept of the tragic hero, that most important of the "better men" who are found in tragedy.

It will be remembered that the tragic hero, like the tragic plot, is usually to be drawn from myth.

...the poets, who did not look for material systematically but in a haphazard fashion, discovered that what they wanted was to be found in the myths; so they needs must rely on those houses, in which such tragic events have occurred.

The value of these mythical themes, in Aristotle's opinion, was partly that they provided examples of greatness and suffering which were appropriate to the best tragedy. We may further assume that Aristotle appreciated the element of "aesthetic distance" which grand characters, drawn from a misty, departicularized, past contributed. We can only assume this, because he does not say it explicitly, and in fact allows that it may be permissible for the tragedian to create non-mythical tragic characters. Yet Aristotle was deeply involved in the mythical tradition for tragedy, and it seems probable that he meant more than he says: that he took the myths for granted, and accepted as a desirable matter of course the "aesthetic distance" which those myths establish between their heroes and men in "real life." This conviction, in Aristotle, would be consistent with what we know him to have believed concerning the exact nature of the tragic hero, that

he is not extraordinary in virtue and righteousness, and yet does not fall into bad fortune because of evil and wickedness, but because of some error of the kind found in men of high reputation and good fortune, such as Oedipus and Thyestes and famous men of similar families.

We may ask ourselves why Aristotle formed this definition. Was he affected, in forming it, by contemporary Greek ethics? Or was he inspired more by aesthetic considerations? A suggestion of the answer can be found in his discussion, in chapter 13, of plots to avoid in tragedy. There he disqualifies three plot themes on the grounds that they do not arouse pity and fear, as does the plot involving the suitable tragic hero. The disqualified plots involve the passage of a good man from good to bad fortune and of a bad man either from bad to good, or from good to bad, fortune. It is significant that Aristotle omits the possibility of a good man passing from bad to good fortune. The point of special interest to us, though, is the "mathematical" aspect of Aristotle's argument. I use the word "mathematical" loosely. Aristotle is concerned with certain sequences of events into which dramatic characters fit. We feel that he has conceived the notion of the sequence as an independent aspect of the play, as an element of plot into which characters may subsequently be fitted, as numbers may be substituted for the x's in an algebraic formula which exists prior to them. This view is supported by his heavy emphasis on plot as the most important element of tragedy, as the soul of tragedy, as a revelation of character, but essentially as action and not character. Of course in the case before us the general form of the character of the tragic hero—his moderate goodness—is already involved in the conception of the sequence which will contain him. Aristotle has not begun with the notion of a kind of plot and then constructed a kind of hero who would be appropriate to that plot. But by his conviction that action is what reveals character, in drama, he has evidently thought of that tragic hero chiefly in terms of what he *does*—that is, in committing a serious error of judgment (*hamartia*), then recognizing his fault, then suffering a reversal of fortune—and not in terms of what he *is*. So that in his very grasp of the tragic hero Aristotle is thinking of action or plot rather than of character.

In this conception of the tragic hero Aristotle was clearly moved more by aesthetic considerations than by contemporary Greek ethical or religious tradition. It is precisely his dynamic, and at the same time partially abstract, understanding of the situation into which the hero "fits," that assures us of his aesthetic motive. He is interested to some extent in the moral end of the tragic sequence—in what it does to refine our feelings. But that end interests him only in terms of a prescribed, almost ritual, sequence of events which subsume character. Aesthetic pattern is clearly being imposed on "real" experience here, a pattern which only the making mind of the artist, not the natural order of reality, could produce.

iii

The belief that art may be a form of aesthetic expression, drawing on somehow "internal" models, rather than an interpretation of an "external, outer" world, takes shape in Aristotle's mind. We have noticed two indications of this belief and should add a third before some final qualifications.

The notions of necessity (τὸ ἀναγκαῖον) and probability (τὸ πιθανόν) play a great part in Aristotle's discussion of the plot of tragedy, that plot into which the tragic hero must "fit." As concepts they are of great present interest; indicating what Aristotle considered the relation between the artwork and the world beyond it. We may also consider the notions of probability and necessity as further suggestions of Aristotle's belief in the aesthetic (or internal) genesis of the work of art. These concepts offer further evidence on our general question.

Aristotle frequently writes of probability as desirable in literature. Often he seems to have no more in mind than what later French critics termed *vraisemblance,* a conformity to expected patterns of existence, as we experience them in real-life. In this vein he writes:

the plots should not be made up of improbable parts; indeed they should above all contain nothing improbable, but if the unreasonable cannot be avoided, it should be outside the plot, as that Oedipus did not know how Laius came to his death. . . .

In making such points, Aristotle omits the notion of "necessity," which he elsewhere couples closely with that of probability. His conception of probability itself often has an external, partly non-aesthetic reference. Yet his notion cannot be reduced entirely to its external intention: Aristotle is not concerned here only with the importance of our normal, everyday expectations as they operate in the experience of art. Rather expectation in life and expectation in art seem to be the same at this point. The artist's satisfaction of our sense of probability is good artistry. In this connection it is interesting to see how subtle a probability Aristotle will allow in art on the basis of life-expectations. In discussing the proper treatment of "character" in tragedy, he writes:

the fourth necessity is that character be consistent. For if a character is not consistent because the man who was imitated was such a character, nevertheless it is necessary that he be consistently inconsistent.

Aristotle's was not the mind to overlook such a subtle, and aesthetically fitting, probability.

In a further development of these thoughts, however, he turns his concepts of probability and necessity—significantly joined—to more specifically aesthetic uses. We see this in his remarks on the poetic universal, in chapter 9. There it is said that poetry portrays what might have happened rather than, like history, what did happen, "what Alcibiades did or experienced." In this sense poetry deals with things in a more "universal" way than history. Then Aristotle continues:

To deal with them (things) universally is to say that according to probability or necessity it happens that a certain sort of man does or says certain things. . . .

"Necessity," here, discloses itself as a potent addition to "probability"; in this passage "necessity," far more than "probability," directs our attention toward the inner structure of the plot. Probability is a Janus-concept for literary criticism; it points simultaneously outward toward the world and inward toward the work. Necessity, as Aristotle offers it, is more un-ambiguously aesthetic. Doubtless he understands, behind it, such life-experiences as those of "what a person of a particular kind must do" or of "what must follow after certain sequences of events." Yet he seems to be considering, in this passage on the poetic universal, principally that aesthetic enchainment of events which he often emphasizes as essential to the tragic plot. His whole conception of that plot is of a persuasive, self-contained whole, no part of which fails to contribute, for-cingly, to that whole. That structural necessity was a formal counterpart to the theme of theological necessity which was also to pervade the drama.

It is no wonder, in this light, that Aristotle releases his notion of necessity into its fullest meaning when he comes to consider what we call "unity of action," or of plot. The in-sistence on that unity, so influential a factor among the so-called "three unities" of later criticism, cannot be tracked to any single passage in Aristotle—although he expresses the idea most concisely in chapter 8—for it is an important im-plication throughout the *Poetics,* recurring whenever there is an insistence on the well-made plot. In chapter 8, though without using the word "necessity," he states most clearly what he means by that element of plot. He writes that

the plot, being an imitation of an action, should be concerned with one thing and that a whole, and [that] the parts of the action should be so put together that if one part is shifted or taken away the whole is deranged and disjoined, for what makes no percep-tible difference by its presence or absence is no part of the whole.

This is Aristotle's most adequate statement of what he means by a "necessary" plot: each part of it demands the rest, and vice versa. Furthermore necessity within the drama has here become a totally aesthetic concept. We are no longer consider-ing that which is necessary in both "real life" and in drama; for Aristotle seems to suggest that such a necessity may not be discoverable in real life. As he says:

a countless number of things happen to one man, some of which cannot be combined with others in a single unit. . . .

Rather the necessity found in good drama appears to be the product of knowing how to write a tragedy, far more than of knowing life. For Aristotle necessity was more fruitful than probability for *aesthetic* consideration. Necessity was that in tragedy in terms of which the organic, sequential character of plot was more significant than the essential character of the tragic hero. That character, in drama, like the very plot of the drama, was constructed aesthetically, in terms chiefly of art, not of life.

iv

I have touched three aspects of Aristotle's poetic theory: each concerned the question of the source of artworks. His "female deer" argument was an ingenious, concise assertion that the model, or source, or origin, of the artwork may not be external but may be either in the outer world mis-seen or in the artist's mind, indeed almost in his imagination. Subsequently I considered two features of Aristotle's literary criticism: first his view of the great man, or tragic hero, in literature, and his steady implication that that man in literature is different from that man in life and is the product of art, of some model in the artist's mind; second a principal feature of the Aristotelian plot, namely necessity, which was of great importance as a means of organizing, and situating, the fiction of the tragic hero. Necessity in art, for Aristotle, seemed to be a purely aesthetic structure, the result of the addition to his work, by the artist, of a kind of articulation and clarity which real life, the external world, did not reveal.

The general point here could have been illustrated by passages in other writings, in the *Rhetoric,* the *Nicomachean Ethics,* the *Metaphysics.* Poetry ($\pi o \acute{\iota} \eta \sigma \iota s$) fell, for Aristotle, under the general class of the "poetic," or "productive" activities of men: its sister activities were "theoretical" and "practical" respectively, the one concerned with knowledge for its own sake, the other with knowledge as a guide to conduct. "Poetic" production, in that broad sense which includes "literature" as we know it, impressed Aristotle as a fundamental, exemplary art. So, for instance, he implies in the *Metaphysics* that the artist is god-like, a setter-in-motion of a new creation (*Met.* 1034a). Nature, he said earlier in that work, has its principle of motion within itself, while "from art proceed the things of which the form is in the soul of the artist" (*Met.* 1032a). That is, art receives its motion from outside, from its creator, while nature, in Aristotle's thought, is a closed system of self-propelling energy. (Though I wonder, here, why motion does not pass from the creator of art into his work as absolutely as from the creator of nature into nature.) This general point about art is summed up in a statement from the *Ethics:*

All art is concerned with coming-into-being, i.e., with contriving and considering how something may come into being. (*Ethics* 1140a.)

In each of these assertions Aristotle sees the artist's creative power as the—rather, as *a*—source of his work.

This is still not to say a great deal. Did Aristotle believe that the artist, as creator, drew exclusively from forms in his own mind? Do our three examples represent the spirit of Aristotle? Certainly not. We need to remember the whole tenor of the *Poetics.* In Aristotle there is constant emphasis on the importance of the external relationships of art. I think here of probability in art, which Aristotle sometimes treats as a binding of the artist and his work to the "outer world." But a broader series of examples is relevant. The entire emphasis on the greatness of tragedy—on its grave action, its significant hero, its consequential effect on the feelings—implies a close relation of the tragedy to "greatness" outside of art. The external affiliation of art is persistently stressed in Aristotle's thinking; even in the examples analyzed at the outset of this chapter, in each of which Aristotle seemed to be probing, rather than baldly stating, the problem of the relation of art to life. To put this point by an exaggerated contrast, there is in Aristotle no trace of the belief which the surrealists expressed, that the artist should create solely in terms of interior models. In his remarks on painting, Aristotle never considers the possibility of a non-representational art. Did he believe that the forms in the artist's mind, to which we have traced them, were in some further sense also drawn from "outer reality"? That the great man, as a form in the tragedian's mind, was at the same time a synthesis, or a crystallization, of great men experienced in life? Or that the tragic flaw, in the drama, essentially sprang from the experience of tragic flaws in life? We can only speculate. Nor does Aristotle say how the elements of life might find their way into art via the artist's mind, or just what kind of transformation they would have to undergo in the process. Much of that tract of inner geography in which "reality," or the experience of reality, is converted into art, remains unmapped in the *Poetics,* as in most theories of poetry. We are left with the feeling that Aristotle, with his public, outwardly conception of drama, found part of the origin of the work of art in the experience of life. We sense that he occupied a transitional position, that he is pushing toward a notion of the independence of art, but has a persistent, unshakable conviction of the closeness of art to life.

Aristotle's honesty—and I think proper complexity—is meaningful. I think it can be even better appreciated, too, in terms of a few historical remarks. The aesthetics of Plato and Plotinus, respectively, will help. I see in the thought of those men, whose speculations lie at the beginning and end of ancient aesthetics, opposed but extreme, exaggerated solutions to the problem of the origin of the artwork.

Plato's attitude to poetry is ambiguous: on the one hand he considers the poet an inspired seer, able to intuit the Ideas directly; on the other hand, the poet for Plato is a second-rate craftsman. These two positions are never reconciled, mainly because of the sterility of the inspiration-doctrine, which would not lend itself to an organic notion of the poet's nature. The doctrine of the poet as craftsman—like saddle-maker or cobbler—interests me here. Plato asserts, for the artist, the primacy of the "thing," of the imitatable object or objects in the "external world." There is a strong "externalizing" movement here, a going-forth to what things are, out-there. In Plato's view those "things" were nearer truth, nearer the Ideas, than any representatives of them could be. As such these "things," and not some refinement or transformation of them in the artist's mind, were emphatically the proper models in his work, and in one way or another deceived his audience into believing that he was showing them reality. This fundamental trickery of art was central in Plato's aesthetic doctrine.

In opposition to Plato's idea of the Primacy of the outer world, for the artist, Plotinus asserted the primacy of the artist's own, self-transcending inner world. Plotinus was responsible to Plato for the main lines of his own thought, and had doubtless learned from Plato's view of the divinely inspired poet. That is, Plotinus certainly used Plato in his effort to surpass him on a particular point of criticism. But the effort to surpass is not less significant. Plotinus believed, in the first place, in the essential oneness of the artist with the natural or outer world. His system of thought is a spiritual monism, in which all things are one by virtue of a single, underlying spiritual substance. That substance is the ground of intelligibility, of all that is, and yet, even in its oneness, exists in different degrees of what we might call self-realization. The Plotinian universe is constructed along a series of diminishing levels of spiritual realization: the line of descent is from the One, through Divine Mind (a kind of activated complex of Platonic-type Ideas), through human mind, until finally it shades off, among the lowest levels of unconscious being, into the most diminished form which spirit can accept without being converted into matter. (Matter, like evil, existing in this system only as a never existent frontier, or limit, of being.) It further characterizes this system that each level in it strives toward the level above it, toward a higher stage of self-realization. Inanimate nature "yearns" to be raised to a higher level, to return toward the source which emanated it. Man "yearns" toward the Divine Mind.

Into this system Plotinus fits the artist and his work. The artist assists nature, the "external world," in its effort to acquire a higher spiritual existence. Thanks to his position, both one with and elevated above nature, the artist is able to intuit those spiritual forms, higher than himself, which are continuous with the nature of the object of the artist's art; then through enacting this intuition, in art, the artist can draw the particular external "object" up toward a higher existence. Not surprisingly, in view of the language of this aesthetic, Plotinus offers his best example in terms of sculpture. He writes:

Suppose two blocks of stone lying side by side, one unpatterned, quite untouched by art, the other wrought into the statue of some god or man, Grace or Muse—a creation in which the sculptor's art has concentrated every loveliness.
Now the stone thus wrought by the artist's hand to beauty of form is beautiful not as stone—for so the crude block would be as pleasant—but in virtue of the form imposed on it by art. This form is in the designer before ever it enters the stone: he holds it not by his equipment of eyes and hands but by his participation in his art.

In Plotinus this "form" which the artist imposes on the stone, or on the natural object in general, is itself a shadow, or essence, of the Beauty in the Divine Mind which the artist is—in a sense—through his experience. We see here how the artist, working down from this form, *imposes* it on his medium. At this point Plotinus' position becomes most relevant to the present argument. The notion that the artist, in assisting the struggles of natural creation toward higher spiritual existence, must intuit transcendent forms, and then draw his natural medium up toward those forms—that involved notion is central in Plotinus' aesthetic. It is a clear counter-position to Plato's assertion of the primacy of the "outer thing" for the craftsman-like artist. The "outer world," the "outer thing," remains, in Plotinus' aesthetic, merely the malleable, though more or less intractable, plasm in which the artist embodies his intuition. The true origin of the art-work, the point at which it begins, is now the experience of transcendent form in the artist's process of creation.

"Between" Plato and Plotinus, on this matter, stands Aris-totle. He held that in many ways the artist creates out of "forms" in his mind, or is at least not restricted to copying forms or objects in the outer world. We are never quite sure how Aristotle understood the nature of these forms in the artist's mind. When Abercrombie refers to them, collectively, as a "conception of life" in the creative mind, we feel no closer to a solution. I prefer to think that Aristotle is working toward a doctrine of imagination, of some sense-unifying, creative principle in mind. Yet we are given no details. We only note the clarity with which Aristotle rebuts Plato here. At the same time that there is, in Aristotle, a potent and origi-nal emphasis on the creativity of the artist's mind as the ori-gin of the artwork, there is a refusal to dissipate the discussion into the empyrean. There is no statement or assumption, in Aristotle, that the artist might draw upon transcendent forms for his aesthetic creations. Aristotle's artist is not a madman; he does not compose in an ecstatic communication with Di-vine Mind. Nor does the *Poetics* offer an image of the artist as a man who draws up nature to utterly new form, trans-forming nature in the strictest sense. There is a strong—and I think sane—"external" reference in the *Poetics*: a reference, through probability, to the structure of real life as experience; and a reference, through the ethical and anthropocentric tenor of Aristotle's aesthetic, to what we might today call the "human condition." Aristotle intends tragedy, we feel, to maintain a firm, self-guaranteeing relation to that "external" situation. Thus he does not, like Plotinus, unambiguously remove the "origin" of the artwork from the outer world. Rather it remains open, in the *Poetics,* that the question of that origin may be extremely involved, that it may concern the complex transaction by which, in poetry, experienced reality is translated into language, is artificialized on the elementary levels of human consciousness. So modern is Aristotle that he forces us to questions which only the most contemporary adventures in depth psychology can begin to answer.